VALENTINE'S VERSE 2005

Edited by

Chiara Cervasio

First published in Great Britain in 2005 by
ANCHOR BOOKS
Remus House,
Coltsfoot Drive,
Peterborough, PE2 9JX
Telephone (01733) 898102

SB ISBN 1 84418 404 8

FOREWORD

Anchor Books is a small press, established in 1992, with the aim of promoting readable poetry to as wide an audience as possible.

We hope to establish an outlet for writers of poetry who may have struggled to see their work in print.

The poems presented here have been selected from many entries, and as always editing proved to be a difficult task.

I trust this selection will delight and please the authors and all those who enjoy reading poetry.

Chiara Cervasio
Editor

CONTENTS

UNTITLED

Blank paper of my heart
I have covered you with
Passions and charms of love
And the scribbling
Of its outbursts
Eager to clothe you with
My ink blots
And entrust
With romantic thoughts
Effusions -
Of my emotions
Ah! Dear heart
But when I review
You -
In your new apparel
I wondered if you looked
Better bare
Then tattered in torment
And melancholic flair

Nayyer Ali Chandella

VALENTINE'S LOVE

V ery much, I love you so
A lways in my heart you know
L et me be the one to win through
E agerly I await your reply
N o, would make me want to cry
T ell me what your heart desires
I will see if mine aspires
N eed to know that you'll be mine
E mbraced in arms entwined

P G H Payne

WANTING AND WAITING

I wish upon a distant star
Defiant and resigned
That though you are so far away
My heart is not yet blind.

I often dream of breaking free
From love's cruel twist of fate
But my soul is bound forever
And you'll never be too late.

I conjecture what the future holds
And hope beyond all doubt
That one day you will come to me -
Your heart will seek mine out.

Until that day I will hold true
I'll wait with bated breath
I never will stop loving you
Not even in death.

Hannah Pay

VALENTINE'S DAY

Let me see a smile on your face dear,
Let the sun from your heart shine through
For just one loving smile, dear
Will take me the whole day through
Take me and hold me, my darling
Let loneliness fly far away
Together we'll stand on the threshold
To watch the sunrise begin a new day.

H Bullough

MORE THAN WORDS CAN SAY

I sit and watch you when you sleep,
You forever I wish to keep,
To be with you is a dream come true,
My feelings are fresh and totally new.

You are everything I dream of and so much more,
You are the fairy tale I've been wishing for,
In a room you stand out in a crowd,
And when I'm with you I feel so proud.

I haven't felt this way in many years,
And even though I have some fears,
I hope the love between you and me
Will be forever, for eternity.

This is where my life does lay,
Because I love you more than words can say.

Sarah J Freeman

WHY ... ?

Questioningly I felt your hand,
A touch to feel if you were cold.
Why then did you not grip mine
In a vice-like hold?

Why did you sit so deep in thought?
That night in January, so late,
When the silence was so loud,
Why did I fail to rouse and conciliate?

Why is it that I cannot think
Which way to turn and see,
The simple signs this silence showed
That maybe you too, were feeling just like me?

Heather Williamson

THE VALENTINE

Each February it arrives
always on time,
across the years, across the seas,
since our bicycle schooldays,
when hands on shoulders,
we pedalled through
the spring.

We parted,
married someone else,
reared our children,
lived in different worlds.

Each year the symbol changes,
two hearts, a love bird,
a girl on a swing;
but the message is the same,
'You're my valentine'.

What is it?
Can't be love,
must be friendship,
or a remembering of
those carefree years
when the soul awakened to
a first romance.

Abina Russell

STRONGER THAN PASSION

Heard your voice no . . .
Not even that.
Was told you called -
It was enough.
Darkness developed
Weightlessness
And soared this
Giggling fantasy
To another plane.
You are inside
This flesh
Enhanced soul,
And, though I may not
Touch, see or
Even know where you
Lay your head
I carry all that was you
In a vault
In my heart,
Never to be released.
For what you showed me
Takes me along this journey
Of life,
With knowledge
Of love.

Denise K Mitchell

VALENTINE

sunset with your fading rays
the moon comes out to shine
our love has stood the test of time
with your hand in mine

sunrise starts another day
your love so strongly felt
in all the years we shared together
my heart you can but melt

so let's continue on our way
along the weary path
hope springs eternal
with a love born from the start

oh valentine arouse my ardour
and give to me a song
violins played sweetly
until the break of dawn

Margery Rayson

WAITING

(Dedicated to my husband Kevin)

I see you every day
We chat as we pass by
You may never know
How my heart pounds so
Or how long I wait
For a sign from you
My valentine.

Norma Griffiths

VALENTINE'S DAY

It is not my favourite day
Of the year, I always feel
Valentine's Day is a day of contest.
A day, which I don't qualify for.
It is one of my loneliest days ever.
I don't have anyone to share
This special day with me.
Seeing people celebrate this
Special day, makes me feel
A knife has just been plunged
Into my heart and twisted.
I feel I am the most unloved person
There is on Valentine's Day.
Not everyone is in a relationship.
Not everyone is sent cards,
Given gifts or taken on a date.
Not everyone is expressed romance
And love.

Jenifer Ellen Austin

WITHOUT YOU
(Dedicated to my husband David)

I can hear the ticking of the clock,
the slow beating of my heart,
the breathing of the wood of my desk.
Apart from you I exist in a vacuum,
suspended where the wheels of time
rotate as slowly as thick old treacle falls from a spoon.
I reach out tentatively to push them forward
to the glorious time when we will
lie naked together again.

Gail Cox

IF YOU COULD FEEL ABOUT ME

If you could feel about me
The way I feel about you
We could rewrite the book of love
And change our fears into something new.

We could rise a wave of happiness
And be two ships of joy
We'd see new treasures before us
Forever to enjoy.

The night sky would be our stage
So we could play among the stars
We'd destroy the myth that:
Women are from Venus
And men are from Mars.

United as one we'd be so strong -
Immune to all diseases;
We wouldn't care what others thought
And those who would do us wrong.

We'd shout from the highest hill,
Run down the valleys green,
Be the biggest lovebug
Anyone has ever seen.

We'd live the longest life
And no one would tear us apart.
We'd silence the unbelievers,
We'd beat with one heart.

And when our time does arrive
There will be no sadness or questions why;
For we'll be eternal stars
Forever illuminating the night sky.

So when the stars twinkle
I will know that it's you
... If you could feel about me
The way I feel about you.

Kenneth Cutts

WHAT CAN I DO?

What can I do my beloved
I'm happy enough
Only when I love you
Only when I see you
As a man I dream about
As my wonderful knight
I'd like to thank you
For your beauty
For your face so sweet to me
For your voice so tender
For the eyes I remember
Were always so joyful to me
I want to dream about you always
My lover from the old days
I'll never forget you my love
Your picture is always above
Every day and every night
I feel your understanding sight
And this is so much to me
It just used to be
Forever

Anna Cellmer

SKIN

When black flows into white;
That multitude of colour,

So many choices when taking a lover.

When brown flows into yellow;
Many shades to find,

There are no divides, other than those of the mind.

As one flows into the other;
The texture of silk;

It's like a human river of honey and milk.

So much love.

David Barnett

GUESS WHO?

At first you were a stranger,
But I'd known you for some time.
You then became my friend,
Through another friend of mine.
You then became my lover,
Although it was, but brief.
We'd broken through the outer shell
And found something beneath.
After our encounter,
We were just friends again.
But since that time, I must admit,
I've never felt the same.
Put two and two together,
And guess who wrote this rhyme?
For I would like so very much,
To be your valentine.

Sue Brown

GIRL IN PINK

What was once a joy is now a chore
We always say good morning, but soon that will be no more.
In its place will be a vacuous smile
And then a nod of the head which is infantile.
Do you remember the times we used to speak?
I do, but the memory is one I care not to seek.
Soon it will be gone for good and so will you,
If only I had the courage to stop and ask you what I want to.
I want to ask you for one day to be my valentine
It would not be anything special, just a meal, candles and
a bottle of wine.
Perhaps you would say yes and hug me tight
Perhaps you would say no and then 'I might.'
It's quite simple though, all you need to do is agree
Unless of course you're the kind of girl who charges a fee.
That would make me think again and probably glance twice
Because, let's face it, you're not that nice.
You dress with style and you always look swell
But you're not the kind of girl to whom I would give the hard sell.
In fact, I'm now having second thoughts about you being my valentine,
Why should I have to pay for the food, flowers and wine?
So don't expect a card from me your highness
There are Jenny and Sarah and Jess for me to bless.
Such is my inertia I cannot even remember your name
What was it now? Rebecca? Catherine? Or Jayne?
It could be something else, but in truth I care not
I'm afraid, my dear, you are long forgot.
But, oh yes, I do remember about you being my valentine,
Are you sure coming to your place is fine?
I'll be round on Monday, see you at nine.

David Dunham

MY VALENTINE

(Dedicated to Bruce, my beloved other half)

My darling Bruce you are my valentine
For 20 years our hearts have entwined
We were not young when we met
But there's a good bit of mileage in us yet
We have lived through scandal and rumour
But have never lost our sense of humour
You always treat me like a lady
You never fail to make me tea
And of you I am most adoring
I must be to put up with your snoring
Thanks to you we have travelled many lands
Always together, holding hands
To me you will always be the sailor boy
Who came into my life and brought me joy
So come on, let's open some champagne and raise a glass
To Valentine's Day, long may our love last.

Marion Kelly

UNTITLED

Hair so fair,
Eyes of blue
I wish I could go training with you
We could run, jump, do press-ups too
I'd be right there beside you
And when we'd been at it for an hour
We could take a bath, or a shower.
I'd wash yours
You'd wash mine
If only you'd be my valentine.

S Biggin

HOME PLANET

Rhyme, rhythm and reason. For what more would I ask
Of those copious, outstretching canopies of a Jeanne Moreau,
For whom the sweet scents of virginity dally still, than to bask
In fitful meditations where pleasures scatter sorrows?

Timing the comfort zone, as laughter in a farce,
Creeps round and round any ivy afterthought. Appreciative
                                                            of tomorrow,
Today, mine is a dry smile rolling from behind a poet's mask,
Onto and over as though the next were but a glance away,
                                                    a dance away, a show

Away from the horizon dancing in the warm summer shimmers
                                                            'de ton mec'.
Those gorged glistenings electrified by your shadow,
A cloak of melodious hues taught to a slender neck

Bursting with passion stolen from a rainbow.
Softly stroked buttocks ooze you in this flow, juice you,
Born in doorways, pulsed with a clue . . . or two.

Ian Lowery

UNTITLED

There is a very special place, deep down inside of me
I keep for my true love, it belongs to him you see
A very special present, he sent to me one day
He said, 'I ask you, sweetheart, don't ever throw it away.'
So now it's all wrapped up, so very tenderly,
Your heart, my true love, is mine for all eternity.

Madeline Wood

GALWAY GIRLS

I fell in love
In Galway
With girls at University College
Decades ago.

I miss Pauline
Dainty and delicate
Her smile and laugh, her lovely face
And her kiss;

But in my mind
My lips on Maeve's
Is the kiss I miss.

To 'The Messiah'
And the London Proms
With tall Annie, bright and fierce Annie
And her kiss;

But in my mind
My lips on Maeve's
Is the kiss I miss.

Frieda the giggler
The cuddler, the leader and singer
The laughter, the lovely lips
I kissed;

But in my mind
My lips on Maeve's
Is the kiss I miss.

Elegant and kind Maeve
A charmer, disarmer, upfront and open.
And in my mind
My lips on yours
Is the kiss I miss, Maeve.

Paddy Murphy

TRUE LOVE

True love is a power
Just give it time to flower
Leaving you in euphoric bliss
Just like your first kiss

Forgive and forget
And you'll have no regret
Just like when your eyes first met

A date with destiny
To make you feel that ecstasy
Keep the sea of love hydrated
And you won't be disappointed

Keep giving and not waiting
True love will see you through dating
Being together is the ultimate high
To depths that you wouldn't believe
A security blanket we all need

That one soulmate who sees you pure
One who you adore

Within them you trust your life
To protect you and keep you from harm
Your lucky charm

Everybody has the chance
For true romance
Keep the love alive and get high
Feel the love and feel it good
Feel the love like you should

Andrea Crome

SOULMATE
(Dedicated to my soulmate, my husband Michael)

Peaceful is my mind
My body at ease
As we walk and wind
Through green leafy trees

Hand-in-hand
With the man I love
Over the beautiful green land
The Lord made from above

We both feel the same
Although no words are spoken
As we start back the way we came
If we weren't together our hearts would be broken.

He is my soulmate
My friend for life
For my love, you'll never have to wait
Till death us do part I'll always be your wife.

Gail Wooton

FOR PAUL

Desire, defeat
Walking is sweet,
Heaven is closer
As I hear the beat . . .

Your footsteps come nearer
My mind gets clearer

This is a lover
I've waited to meet . . .

All my life.

Anita Ann McNamee

SHARE AND DREAM

(Dedicated to Phil, the love of my life
Very happy Valentine's Day, cheers, Jan xxx)

By chance they met in London
Both from different parts of the country
And yet working for the same company
Both on different training courses
It was raining and glances were exchanged
Would you like to share my umbrella?
And they shared
Can I take you out for lunch?
And they shared the bill.
Will you share my life in London?
And they shared
Marry me and share all my dreams
And they dreamt
32 valentine years on, and many more dreams later
They still share and dream.

Jan Gray

THE FIRST DAY

From the very first day we met
I knew you were the one for me
That look in your eye
How could I ever forget
How you looked after me?
You're the only one for me.

You lift me up when I feel down,
Always bringing a smile to my face
You're my only inspiration
Throughout my whole life.

You'll be my everlasting,
You are my everlasting love.

Sarah Grigor

17

REVIVED WITH A KISS

Your satin lips raise rich flowers of warmth to my cold skin
with an ever love-sealed smile you kiss me and as
your cherished eyes weave through my thoughts with delicacy
I worship every breath that passes through me, while in your embrace.

Beneath the moon's silver ray of Heaven's song, I watch you sleep.
And when you wake and help me stand, you vanquish all darkness
snapping at my heels.
And I feel my soul merge with shimmering hues into yours,
enlightening my existence.

Your alluring beauty flickers from within your spirit,
as you embrace my supple body.
Your sensuous voice lets precious rubies blossom in my heart.
And as you draw my lips to yours, the eternal flame of Love
revives my life
Which was lost within an ominous ocean.

Jessica Stapleton

ODE TO MY LOVE

My husband, Mick, is my valentine true
For my love for him is never overdue
His presence in my life is so unique
For life without him would be so bleak.

He's my friend, my soul, my lover
Why would I need any other?
For only without him my life would suffer
So please take heed, I don't want any other.

My poem may be simple
I'm sure you'd agree
But he's the only man
Who can really satisfy me!

Jane Beresford

ONLY YOU

I have asked myself a thousand times
Why it has to be you, and no one else
I never listen to what my heart tells
It can only be you . . . and no one else . . .

I always waited for that prettier girl
With dimpled cheeks and darling smile
She would talk in a whisper . . . walk with a swirl
For her, I should wait a little while
But, to me, what beauty spells . . .
It can only be you . . . and no one else .. .

I see her stepping barefooted
On the dew-laden grass of a green meadow
I see her radiance enchanted
Pure . . . divine . . . innocence of a dove
Dancing with the waves and gazing wide-eyed
I see her gathering seashells . . .
It can only be you . . . and no one else . . .

I have many a story to share with you
And there's so much more to hear too
What have we been talking about all this while
Now won't you tell me that little tale
Of divine love . . . and wedding bells
It can only be you . . . and no one else.

Vivek Parameswar Sarma

A VALENTINE'S MESSAGE

Saint Valentine's tradition, so many years ago
Bestowed on us the gift of love, and opened up the door,
To love and understanding, the meaning of romance,
Like Romeo and Juliet, true love is now enhanced.
A time to show your loved ones, how much you really care
For all those lasting memories, and happiness you share.
People of all ages, the young and very old
Still celebrate this special day, with love worth more than gold.
Two hearts that are forgiving, and always understand
One who walks the second mile, and never makes demands.
These special hours are precious, romance is all around,
Cupid shares this day with you, much happiness is found.

I'd give a very special gift, on this romantic day
To fill your heart with happiness in each and every way.
I'd fill a day with fragrance, the perfume of a rose,
And tie this gift with rainbows, with love that grows and grows.
A basket filled with shining stars, to shine for you each night
Would make your world a better place of wonder and delight.
I'd scatter sunbeams on your path, to warm each breeze that blows,
All of these are gifts of love, more than you'll ever know
Where willows droop to water, and birdsong fills the air,
This day will be so perfect, without a single care.

Saint Valentine, he brought romance to every single heart,
He brought us joy and happiness, true love could never part.

Marjorie J Picton

SURE

I was young, unsure of myself, when . . .
First I saw his back,
Back of his neck,
Dark hair, cut square,
Stiff collar on fawn shirt,
Tie done tight.
Glimpsed dancing eyes in the mirror.
I smiled, he grinned.
A few short days decided us,
We were sure we'd stay together.
In those wondrous days with him, his love surrounded me.

There came a time when I believed
Love had deserted me
My mouth was parched, my mind a void.
The pain surrounded me,
Some day I thought, I will be sure.

He gives so much, this man I love.
What can he see in me?
In my mirror I see lines and wrinkles, greying hair,
Belly sagging, flabby arms, but . . .
His eyes reflect his love for me
As he reaches for my hand,
He holds me fast and strokes my arm.
I'm loved by him, sure of him,
Moved by his love.

C M Richardson

MY LOVE

Love is devotion,
Also an emotion,
My heart is for you,
And is so true,
Love to me is,
Caring and sharing,
Grinning and bearing,
Good times and bad.

Your eyes are like crystals,
So pure and true,
Oh what a joy to be with you,
Your touch is divine,
How lucky am I for that to be mine,
May our love last forever,
Our hearts stay together
Forever and ever.

Rebecca Tombs

VALENTINE

Oh sweet Valentine
I wish you were mine
If only you could see
How much you mean to me
As I look from afar
How dear to me you are
Oh sweet Valentine
These words I write to you
As my feelings over time just grew
So I give you my heart
Sweet Valentine never to part
If only you knew
This love I feel so true.

Maggie Strong

MY VALENTINE

Did we ever care . . .
Did we ever love . . .
Did we ever fear . . .
That we'd let it go . . . ?

Our little dream
And all we shared . . .
Suddenly - so quick,
Out in the blue, all disappeared . . .

Still
You'll always be . . .
Now . . . and all future
Months of February,
My love -
A special valentine
To me . . .

Jorunn Ingebrigtsen

A POEM FOR MUM

Eyes blue as sky,
Lips like dye,
Hair really light,
Eyelashes like night,
Necklace all gold,
Earrings all bold,
Have you guessed
Or have I messed?
Yes, all right, it's correct
It's my beautiful mum.
　　　She's great!

Hannah Atkinson (10)

VALENTINES IF I MUST!

It is time for love or so you tell me,
It's time for flowers, chocolates and cards;
I don't do that, I can't be a***d you see,
So I've written this sonnet like past bards.
I do love your smile and your golden hair,
Your eyes so blue, so pure like summer days.
I admire the way you will always share,
I'm still amused when you sing 'Purple Haze'.
You remind me how to be a good guy,
You suffer in silence when I'm a fool,
Put up with my antics with but a sigh;
When I've been a burk, you tell me I'm cool.
'Love You' is something I really should tell,
There is no card, but this sonnet was hell.

Marty Grief

NO LONGER TO DREAM
(Dedicated to Michelle Cloarec-Pollard, my wonderful wife)

The first day that I saw you, my heart missed beat,
My mouth went all dry when I tried to speak,
My eyes glassed over when on you they did descend
That magical moment I wanted never to end

A voice of an angel when you said hello,
Shaking my hand, I was thinking, please don't let go!
On our first date we walked along Rhododendron Mile
And all I could see was your innocent smile.

Time has moved on, now we're husband and wife
And because you are with me I have a wonderful life
I want for nothing, all I need, my love, is you
No longer do I dream, because my dream has come true.

Christopher Cloarec-Pollard

UNTITLED

If you were here I'd hold you,
Hold you close as close could be . . .
I'd lightly stroke the small of your back,
And trace my fingers around your lips . . .
I'd breathe you in and cherish your sweet scent,
Devote myself to you completely,
Know you in totality . . .
So the next time we're apart
I'd have more of you to remember . . .

Jason Whitehall

OUR TEACHER'S VALENTINE'S CARD

Our teacher's got a valentine card
He thinks that we don't know
But we are quick to spot
How his face is all aglow.

He thinks we cannot see
The way he trembles with the chalk
He thinks we haven't noticed
His funny little walk.

He thinks he's kept it quiet
And we haven't worked it out
But on this occasion
There isn't any doubt.

For what really blew it,
What gave the game away
Is simply that it was our class
Who sent it anyway!

D Sheasby

ENOUGH

Morning reaches out
Between the closed blinds
Into our room.
I lie, not quite awake,
Resisting the day, yet
Too scared to sleep lest the moment is missed.
You breathe slowly,
Unaware that I am aching for you
To open your eyes and love me again.
We lie together
So close that our skins melt as one.
Yet, still not close enough to satisfy.
You stir, a restless animal
Innocent in your dream.
I miss you and touch your lips with mine.
The moment is here
Your eyes, strong and clear
Fix on mine.
Almost satisfied, not quite.
Is there more?
You love me, give everything
But the body needs more
The heart demands more.
Can you give enough
For me?

Carrie Ruxton

FOR TRACEY

A rose may be red
And a violet may be blue
But a flower of any colour
Is pale in comparison to you.

Lee Cobb

HEART AND SOUL

When all seems lost,
lost in a lost world,
she smiles and her warmth,
warms my lonely heart,
her sweet love guides me,
finds me.
She loves me, heart and soul.

When all seems pointless,
pointless in a pointless world,
she holds me and her love,
gives me a reason
to believe.
I love her, heart and soul.

When life feels so sad,
in a sad, bad world,
I see her, I hear her,
and then the world is
alright with me,
you see,
she gives me her heart and soul
she is with me everywhere I go.

Will McTavish Martin-Grayston

TOGETHER

Thinking of my love.
He is my epicentre.
I am his shelter.
Together we brave the storm
then we walk in the sunshine.

J P Henderson-Long

YOUR VALENTINE

I'll always be your valentine.
Your eyes have never lost their shine,
these forty years, my Columbine,
these short years that I've called you mine.
Your eyes have never lost their shine,
nor mine, when mine and yours combine.
These short years that I've called you mine
have been my very bread and wine,
for when my eyes and yours combine,
it seems we each on other dine.
You've been my very bread and wine,
the products of life's wheat and vine.
It seems we each on other dine,
as every day our thoughts entwine.
The product of life's wheat and vine
sustain us, should our luck decline,
as every day our thoughts entwine
to bring us hope, and all is fine.
We are sustained, should luck decline,
for love creates its own design:
it brings us hope, and all is fine.
All else to elsewhere we consign.
As love creates its own design,
we never may from love resign.
All else to elsewhere we consign.
For forty years I've called you mine.
We never may from love resign.
I'll always be your valentine.

Adrian Brett

NORMAN

Many years ago - at a very early age
I first met Norman on the pantomime stage
Boys and girls in our early teens
Trying our skills doing pantomime scenes.

We'd been guides and scouts - then the youth club
Not much money or time to spend in the pub
Teens led to twenties and careers that led
To foreign lands, some went alone, some wed.

Then over fifty years later - in fact, last May
We had a 'panto' reunion - what a happy day
I went on my own, my husband had died
Many years ago - so to look my best I tried.

A new hairdo and outfit gave me some courage
And also I hoped - portray a good image.
There were many faces that I knew well
And lots of stories and events to tell.

Someone whispered to me - 'Norman's wife passed away
A few years ago - so glad he could come along today.'
I looked up, our eyes met - he asked, 'Like a drink?'
'Oh, yes please!' I replied - he smiled and gave a wink.

'Let's sit over there - catch up on times gone by.'
So we talked and laughed, even had a little cry
No tears in the future - we mean to have a good time
Thanks to the reunion of 'Pals of the Pantomime'.

Pamela L Davies

TO LOVE AGAIN

I said I could not love again, be close to anyone.
I could not face the breaking up that follows all the fun.

I would not lose my heart again, have faith in any man -
To want, to yearn, to dream of love as only lovers can.

I said I could not go through life with my heart upon my sleeve
To look in someone else's eyes, to want, or to believe.

How could I now with all my years relive the youthful joy.
Romancing like a schoolgirl just meeting her first boy?

But love can be as tender in age as much in youth
If one can only just believe that some can tell the truth.

Is time so changed? Am I a fool to think that love can bloom
That I can still feel happy when someone walks in the room?

We lose our inhibitions as time goes marching on
For time is short, we don't pretend and youth is so soon gone.

So now this can't be girlish fun that brings its joy and pain
It must be deeper down than that to think it's love again.

Helen E Utting

UNCONDITIONAL LOVE
(Dedicated to my husband, Darren)

At times you are so grumpy.
You're smelly and you're old.
Time has not been kind to you as you are going bald.
But I feel, dear Darren, that you need to be told
That you're my dearest sweetheart and your heart is made of gold.
I love you more than words can say and hope that you love me.
You're my special valentine and always will be.

Cheryl Arnold

A POEM FOR ST VALENTINE'S DAY

The day's history goes back to 240 AD, that's many a year,
It has not always been full of love and joy though, I fear.
The day we give flowers, cards, gifts, and have done over history,
Has an intriguing story, dark, cold and shrouded in mystery.
There are three Saint Valentines, all of them martyrs too,
All three died on February the 14th, thank God, not me or you.
Valentine, a priest, beheaded for marrying lovers in secret,
Against Emperor Claudius' wishes, who sadly did suspect.
Valentine fell in love with his jailer's daughter, visiting him,
Before death he wrote her: 'From your Valentine' - not a whim.
The day was also the pagan Lupercalia fertility festival,
The priests would sacrifice a goat, a dog or any other animal.
The priests gathered in the cave of infants Romulus and Remus,
Where they had been well nurtured by a she-wolf or Lupus.
It was also the day on which birds were supposed to pair,
For our beautiful fauna brethren, love was also in the air.
The first card was in 1415 by Charles, Duke of Orleans, to his wife,
It's in the British Museum, and outlived the love of his life.
In 1840 Esther A Howland first sold cards in mass production
The most expensive from Onassis to Callas; emeralds, diamonds.
Now it's the day on which lovers or sweethearts, well chosen,
Are given chocolates and red roses, preferably a dozen.
The day on which big red hearts and bigger gifts abound,
A day for which adverts in every shop and newspaper are found.
For those with someone to love, the day is sublime,
But for the bereaved and lonely, it can be a tough time.
There are poets who have praised it; Gower, Brews, John Lydgate
The poetry within us all would like us to find our eternal mate.
For me, love and joy on St Valentine's are my true fate,
My dear new husband's name is very truly John Ludgate!

Mary May Robertson

SNUGGLED CLOSE . . .

A warm glow within my heart
tells me you're the other part
of my soul, the vital piece
that makes me whole . . .

With this in mind I strive
to be kind and good.
Do those little things,
that I know I should.

And when you smile
in that certain way,
that's when I want to stay
snuggled close, on Valentine's Day!

Joanne Manning

LOST LOVE

Where is he now?
Many years have passed
Since I saw him last,
Will he remember this day?
With a card, I pray?
Not handsome at all,
A kind heart I recall.

Enriched by his voice,
Just allow me a choice
Of a voice or a card,
Conveying his regards
To a long lasting 'stray',
On this St Valentine's Day.

Barbara R Lockwood

EARTH

The lips brush the skin like a breeze
Drifting over contoured earth;
Seeking the folds, the corners that lie secretly -
The verdant dell or foliate clough -
And the divisions that fall between.
The curve is inward from the spine
Its long chain forming a slender bridge
Across the hourglass of the back.
Two hands can meet from the thumb tips
With fingers that complete a circle round the waist,
Measuring the attribute where nature
Has provided a lean valley and allowed
A knowledge of that fulsome earth.
The bones have cracked to the kiss,
To the wild breath - bringing
The limb gently through the recoil.
Its resistance not held against
The strengthening caress - but released
Like blossom from its linkage,
With that petal from the moistened lip.

William Birtwistle

GEMINI LOVE

I like it when you're near me
You make me feel new -
Shining as the silvered morning dew
I like the feel of you -
And no matter what we do or say -
In the early light we get up
And go our separate way
And gamble three twice plus eleven
On a given day.

Colin Zarhett

LOVE

Love is a mixture of emotions
You think you love someone
But then you find that person
Is not the one for you.

It is a roller coaster of ups and downs
You can't make up your mind
You feel strange and funny
You have to pick up that thread
But you don't know where to begin.

You don't understand what is happening
How can you feel so much for that person?
Then you decide you don't have any feelings at all
For that special someone.

It is like a ship without an ocean
Or music without any song
How do you decide between right and wrong
Without hurting someone's feelings
Or making the wrong decision?

No one knows the answer
You just have to follow your heart in the end.

S Langridge

DUSTY

You wake me up each morning
And take me for a walk
You're the best friend that I have
But I wish that you could talk.

Emily Marlborough

TRUE HAPPINESS
(Dedicated to my husband, Bob, for all his love and support over the years)

Do you remember when we first met,
and gradually our two lives became entwined?
The heart would quicken at the sound of your step
your smile would brighten even the dullest day.
Gradually we settled into marriage and children,
and the years gently rolled on.
Like all couples we have faced life's ups and downs
we've known some sadness, but mainly just happiness.
By today's standards we have little wealth
but I would have to beg to disagree.
We have life's most treasured gift,
a wealth of love for one another.
What could be more precious than that?
True happiness can never be bought
it comes from the love we have for one another.

Zandra Collisson

UNTITLED

I love you today and every day
in a unique and special way
I could have been a princess
beautiful too
but I became Fiona cos
I married you
so when you look at me
and think I'm a wreck
remember I gave up my princes
for Shrek.

Gina Stokes

A LOVER'S BABBLE

My beloved, my honey, I say,
This heart throbs for you night and day,
But there's none to show the way,
How to cross this thorny bay.

The day will come I always dream,
When you and I would live supreme,
Far from those who ridicule and hate
The heavenly marriage of *love* and *fate*.

Beside the hills and by the streams,
Where life is filled with joy to the brim,
And where people love till death,
All the while with soul and faith.

And all I want is love from you,
To glitter my life like a dew,
To the very end and to the last,
Till this body of mine returns to dust.

I hope the past you do recollect,
When life hadn't many adjectives to choose from or select,
When love meant sweet ignorance and carefree indulgence,
And every sorrow was profound, every joy dense.

Yet I know not how this billet-doux could conclude,
Without me getting stupid and perhaps lewd,
For I must tell you the amorous theme,
That is the crux of my every sweet dream!

Shivaji K Moitra

TWO HEARTS ENTWINED

Two hearts entwined,
Together as one,
They share life's experience,
They share all life's fun.

They share all life's burdens,
All the pain and the strife,
But the power of their love,
Will carry them far in life.

Always there for each other,
Unfailing in their faith,
Each heart know it's found,
Its one true soulmate.

I used to wonder if one day,
A girl would steal my heart,
And now that I've found you,
I can't bear us to be apart.

It's a wonder how two hearts,
Can beat together as one,
Yet their love still shines brightly,
Like the rays of the sun.

For two hearts entwined,
Forever as one,
A bond never broken,
Not by anyone.

Pete Robins

EXPRESSION OF LOVE IN MANY WAYS, WITH A ROSE

If I were to give you a fresh burgundy rose
Which compares flowing beauty and that of prose
And what if it were a delicate shade of pink
What grace and gentility you have, I think.
The orange and coral and all that is floral
The desire to love you even though immoral.
A room adorned with a bouquet made of yellow
Pure joy you give me, being your play-fellow.
The puritanical brilliance of a rose that is white
Embellishes the worthiness of my love's might.
Sweetheart roses be my darling, honey, my dear
When love is strong and in ascent, have no fear.
Harmonious sight, the red and white together
Love you till eternity with passion that is red.

The perfect way to say I love you, with a rose.
To you, my dear, lovingly from me.

Rashid Ali

LOVE

Love has no expiry date
Love opens dreams and imagination
Love sparkles through each heart
Love brings the magic that one longs for
Love knows no boundaries
Love can shine and make you feel invisible
Love is a potion that you find
A very rare potion
But when you have it, it's difficult to separate it
From reality
It's the greatest degree one can accumulate
Other, the years
Love is all one can remember you by.

Ines Newell

THE DREAM OF BIG LOVE

The strong wind blows from mountains,
The wasp wheels round a bunch of grapes,
With clanging wings!
The eagle wheels under the clouds
Flying in his habitual way
Looking for suitable prey!
Hunting birdie,
The snake twines round a tree
And ivy twines round a window,
But the hand of a young man,
True gentleman,
Cannot wind around the girl's waist,
His sunlight,
Try as he might!
Therefore the young man,
Suffers from absence of love,
From the absence of the tender dove!
Is it the life?
Hence it's the life without sense!
But the happiness does not come,
However you call it, by gum!

Petr Nicolayevich Maltsev

MY DARLING

I gently kiss her as she sleeps
I wipe her tears away when she weeps
The dawn awakes my one true love
The sun shines down on her from above
I adore her so much I cannot explain
God help anyone who causes her pain
I hold her in my warm embrace
As I look down at my daughter's face.

Julie Owen

TO JOY

The wheel of life has circled round
And favoured us with love profound
From those past days when we were young,
And other lovers shared our song.
We stand on the edge of earthly strife
With vistas of a god-given life,
Of love renewed.

Long or short our time may be
From here until eternity.
Savouring each moment, we will go
Hand in hand, for we now know
That we have found our heart's desire:
Our hearts will ever be afire
With love imbued.

Joy in my heart at your morning greeting,
Ours is the joy of a true lover's meeting;
Your life and mine combined, however fleeting.

Arthur Moore

I LOVE YOU

When you look at me, and I look at you
With ruby lips and eyes of blue
What can it be between you and me?
That we enjoy each other's company.

Is it the flowers that bloom, or the birds that sing
Or is it the fact, that it is spring
That we feel and act the way we do
Then whisper to each other, 'I love you.'

T Gibson

THE IMAGINARY LOVE LETTER TO CASSIO FROM BIANCA

My dearest Cassio,
Please forgive my manner
To myself, my thoughts and feelings for you
I can keep no longer
I must confess I have been very hesitant in writing to you
For you, Cassio, my feelings and love are truly deep in my heart
I cannot bear for us any longer to be apart

'Do you feel contempt of me Cassio?'
If this is so I know then your heart is not with me
I will slip away from thee
I must know if you truly love Desdemona?
As devious Iago strongly doth imply
If this is the situation then I am deeply jealous
I will slip away from you and die

You have been away from me, Cassio, too long
For you my feelings are certainly very strong
You tell me that you have feelings and concern for me
Yet you refused to escort me all the way home
For fear of your general seeing you with me
Cassio, to have full proof of the depth of your love
Feelings and concerns for me, 'Wilt thou wed me?'

M Wood

UNTITLED

Love's timeless message
Sent in anonymity
Pleading cognizance.

Brian Ellis

NATASHA'S MOON

A photograph, a glimmer, a shining star of light
From visual to voice, and then so personal by night
With such a curvaceous joy, of crisp and golden wonder
Heaven is fresh and rests in peace, by you in deepest slumber.
Born within an angel's grace, so sensual and elegant to face
With life so clean within, the seeping heart of your warm kin
Upon its foundations formed and tender, folded wet beneath
The open glide of meeting you, by table not by sheath
Has made this day an endless tale of whirly, hungry whispers
Sweet candy and romance, of you sailing with me in dance
And more may make the spinning top, the bunnies bounce
When the kitten hops across the chairs with balls of wool
Fluffy cotton and realms of spool, when chattering with eyes
You are the darling of this, my wedded Valentine's prize
To kiss and not to miss, to be there for eternity
A spellbound book of roots and wand, to you my love does bond.

Don Capo

SOAPY STUFF
(For Nick)

i love you because of your smile
i love you because i can make you smile
i love you because of the bus trips we shared
   to out-of-town jumble sales, when we were quite new
i love you because you took off my jumble clothes
   after late cinema nights when we were still quite new
i love you because we have always eaten well
i love you because we have never drunk too much
i love you because you make it easy to believe
i love you because i can't rely on the villa
i love you because your babies are beautiful
i love you because you are beautiful
i love you because i feel all this while cleaning the bath

Beck Brookes

VALENTINE PET

(Dedicated to my husband, David - special in every way and forever my best friend)

I don't want a card embossed with a dove
Or a bouquet of roses as proof of your love
No bleeding heart or Cupid with bow
A chocolate box or a candlelit show

I don't want a text or a public display
With a poetic rendition in a Romeo way
No sexy white satin and silk underwear
Or black velvet box with a gold solitaire

I don't want champagne or a soft fluffy bear
Or theatre seat tickets with money to spare
No message displayed and tied to a plane
Or soppy love tokens, they'd drive me insane

All that I want is a smile and a kiss
Your true understanding is heavenly bliss
Valentine, you will be mine 'til the end
Always my true love, forever my friend.

Joyce Graham

WHEN DO I LOVE YOU?

I love you in the summer when the sun is burning bright,
I love you in the winter when the snow is gleaming white.
I love you in the night-time when it's too dark to be seen,
I love you at dinnertime and all times in-between.

I love you when the hedgehog comes tripping through the grass,
I love you when the elephant comes thundering thro' the pass.
I love you when the buffalo come tearing 'cross the plain,
And I love you when the buffalo come tearing back again.

Del Isaacs

REVERIE

(Dedicated to Elaine Pierce, Edinburgh)

your hair
shapes
patterns in hearts

your lips
fashion
curves of desire

your voice
soothes
past scars

your breath
whispers
hints of acceptance

your arms
encircle
the safety of embraces

your walk
attracts
journeys of wonder

your body
fulfils
mutual needs

your scent
drives
moments into madness

your touch
reassures
life is worthwhile

your eyes
melt
the moon into stars

Michael Fenton

TO YOU

The ache that pulses through my being
each time I look upon you seeing
one so gentle, one so fair,
your smiling face, your lovely hair.

I long to see you, yearn to touch
I need you, need you, oh so much.

Each time I look into your eyes
they reflect the beauty of the skies.
The sun, the moon, shine from above
and seem to light my deepening love.

Your presence sweeps all cares away
I want your nearness every day.
You are my soul, you are my life.
I love you so, my darling wife.

To you from me.

John Bryant

VALENTINE
(With love to Jane)

Let me tell you most of all, you, girl, are so beautiful to me
don't be taken by the past, our love will always last

As we travel through in time, falling in love with a girl
in mind, asking a question I don't have to mention to you

Love, love, love, love, when I say these words to you
darling, you know it's very true that I love you

There's no end to the end of the road, there's only
the light of love to follow, will it be today or tomorrow?

Love, love, love, love, I say these words to you in time
we both know it's fine, you are my sweet valentine.

David Williamson

VALENTINE

Fair of hair, angelic face
      A person of beauty, also grace,
Radiant smile, heart full of love
      Dainty and warm, like that of a dove.

To see her makes my knees go weak
      To share her love is all I seek,
Deep down this can never be
      She loves another and is not free.

Yet! Just to look, I mean no harm
      To watch with awe at all that charm,
So dream I shall of future times
      If only, if only she could be mine!

David Richards

SIT WITH ME:
(Poem for a wedding)

I used to sit here on my own, gazing out at life
Watching as the seasons flew, seeing things were 'nice'.
Winter came with spiky frost. Summer tanned my skin.
Looking out was fine by me . . . with no one looking in.

Yet all I knew was torn apart one special, special day.
Someone sneaked up next to me when I glanced the other way.
I fought at first this change of scene, 'I don't need no one,
I like it sitting on my own, being solo makes me strong.'

Yet, bit by bit, my feelings changed, the ice began to melt
I liked the thought of someone there, caring how I felt.
Sharing thoughts, swapping smiles, sheltering the weather
The caring warmth of someone's trust, the strength of being together.

So side by side we cross this land, strengthened by our bond
Treading forth through sunlit glades, enjoying what's beyond.
Colour burst into my soul, my head with gladness spun
Trees planted close are we, our branches twined as one.

I used to sit here on my own, gazing out at life
Watching as the seasons flew, seeing things were 'nice'.
But now, with you, we gaze outside with riches at our feet
I'll love you forever with all my heart, with you my life's complete.

Chris Martin

VALENTINE

When I send my lass a valentine,
My name I'm not allowed to sign.
How will she know that it is me
Wants her, my valentine to be?

When she gets my card by the post
To say that I love her the most,
It will drive me to despair,
If I find she does not care.

If she thinks my card's absurd,
I'll need to find another bird.
Maybe I should get another two,
And tell them all I love them true.

The things I'll do to get a cuddle,
Send my plans all into a muddle,
I'll feel that things will not be bad,
If someone sends to me a card.

Not like the card I got last year
That fairly filled my heart with fear,
To say my gas would soon be cut,
If this bill, was not paid up.

I'll send some cards to myself,
And sit them up upon the shelf.
As there's no signatures to see,
They'll never know they're all from me.

I W Wilkinson

MY VALENTINE

(Dedicated to all the 'Spiky People' out there who find it difficult to show their true feelings and are even afraid to put an arm around the shoulder of someone in trouble)

I hide behind a wall or tree
for you to pass so close to me,
I see your eyes and hear your voice
my loving heart cries out, 'Rejoice.'

In sun or rain I take my place
and hope to see your smiling face,
maybe some day you'll smile at me
and help to easy my misery.

I've learned to love you more each day
I love you more than flowers can say,
I want to touch that face and nose
perhaps some day I'll touch your toes.

A distant love you'll always be
so please, oh please, come close to me,
press Cupid's arrow through my heart
and never ever let us part.

Please will you be my valentine -
I am a little hedgehog and you're a porcupine,
please help me show our two-legged friend
when animals break hearts - they rarely ever mend.

Jim Pritchard

AN EVOLVING ROMANCE

Flattery,
With a smattering of gifts
Is nice, it cannot be denied,
As is champagne chilled in ice.
Flowers, romance, candlelight too
Are fine. But they are not you.

You drive a fast car
Have expensive hi-fi.
You tell me that you expect to fly high.

And I think of the peacock's
Shivering and lovely display.
And the hens all say:
'Look at the tail on that!
He must be a bit of all right . . .'

But for me display obscures intimacy.
I am not so interested in gifts,
Rather in words.
I want to know who you are
Not what you can provide.
Please don't show me things which hide
The delight of discovering
If we can be friends.

So give me yourself
For you never know how far
We could go with words.
And the display?
Trust me. It's strictly for the birds.

Jenny Donnison

UNTITLED

(Dedicated to my wife who has put up with me for 49 years so far)

Will you be my valentine?
You silky, lovely lass,
Rushing past my window
Each day I see you pass.

Your flowing hair streams out behind
As golden as the sun,
Your striding legs are firm and fine
As on your way you run.

On sunny days you saunter
But you never look my way,
Head held high you gaze ahead
Your hips, they gently sway.

Let me shower you with flowers
Of soft and tender hue,
Though none of them can compare
With the beauty that is you.

Let me take you out to dine
With fine food and luscious wine,
Perhaps you'll fall into my arms
And say you will be mine.

I want you and I need you
For ever and a day,
Not just a fleeting moment
As you pass along my way.

But if you should refuse me
I don't know what I'd do,
Unless you have a sister
Who looks as nice as you.

Brian Daulton

POPPY LOVE
(To Alistair, the unattainable!)

'He loves me, he loves me not'
She blows the snowdrop bloom
But pristine petals, pure and white
Will not fall too soon

Frustrating their frigidity
She pulls them one by one
'He loves me, he loves me not'
Till every one is gone

Dissembled and denuded
With just a core of green
She wishes that she'd waited
To find what might have been

Maybe when spring is over
And summer takes a bow
She'll blow a scarlet poppy
'He loves me, loves me now!'

V Jean Tyler

LIGHTHOUSE

You stand out, yes,
you, like a lighthouse,
even now, seen from afar
and from the outside.

Each wink of your eyes
was a warp in the day,
the fall of a star,
a flash of eternity.

Christina Egan

GRANDMA, SING ME BACK

(Dedicated to my favourite angel, who's still my best valentine)

Grandma, sing me back to yesterday.
Hold me in your arms, and hear me say,
'I love you . . .' one more time!

Gaze at me with your sparkling eyes.
Tell me stories while we're baking pies.
Let your voice *ring* through my day.

Grandma, sing me back to yesterday!

I wanna cuddle by the fire and eat ice cream.
Sit around the table and recite our dream.
We could even go out to play!

We could bask on the porch and paint our toes.
Race to the garden and see what grows.
Lord, I'm missin' you today!

Grandma, sing me back to yesterday.
Hold me in your arms and hear me say,
'I love you . . .' one more time!

Holly DeLaughter

MY MAN

How he does love me, I can count the ways
He carries my shopping and tightens my stays
He's kindness personified, stiflingly so
I can't even cough and he won't let me go

But how I do love him, infuriating man
For I know his intentions are good and the plan
Is to lighten my burdens and love me the more
I'll not kick him out, nor show him the door.

Boppy

YOU ARE

You are the life force running through my veins
the healing hand that heals my pain

My day, my night, my moon, my sun
my saving grace when the day is done

My ears to listen when I do not hear
my courage in times when I feel fear

My eyes to see when the day is bleak
my firm support when I feel weak

You are every breath I take
the snow-white swan upon the lake

My golden daffodils that bloom in spring
the only song I want to sing

You are my fire on a winter's morn
my evening sunset, my break of dawn

You are my lover, my best friend
I give you my heart
until my life does end.

Dawn Colley

FOR YOU MY VALENTINE
(Dedicated to my valentine, Keith Moys)

One day we met and fell in love
Which changed our lives, it's true
I always dreamed one day, I would find
A man to love like you

My dreams came true
We fell in love and here we are today
It's obvious that I cannot hide
The love for you I feel inside

I want to shout and tell the world
How much you mean to me
Inside my heart beats forever in time
For you, my darling, my valentine

Time has passed and still I feel your tenderness and love
I know that it will stay this way
Our love will never fade away
As our hearts entwine, it's yours and mine
Always and forever
My valentine.

Christine Noah

You

Sometimes I feel so down
I wonder why I'm here
But something reminds me of you
Then it's clear . . .

I need you, your love
I need to know you're there
I need to hold you, kiss you
I need to know you care . . .

Without you I am incomplete
My mind and body a shell
You give me strength
When all is not well

I want you so badly
So much it makes me cry . . .
The thought of losing you
Just makes my heart die . . .

Juliet Jones

Valentine's Day

Without your love,
The sun won't shine,
All sadness fills,
This heart of mine,
All could be changed,
The sun would shine,
If you would be,
My valentine.

Mary Hughes

SOMETHING EXCITING

Something exciting
missing from my life
- something exciting

Looking for a man
looking for a wife
- someone enticing

Searching on the net
haven't found him yet
- sometimes delighting

Yearning for that touch
words can say so much
- sometimes inviting

Sending out a sign
some day you'll be mine
- unwitting valentine . . .

Julia Murphy

ESSENCE OF LOVE

Squeeze the last drop of me
Melt I to we
Dent your soul
Sweet, tender and whole
You're all that I yearn
The essence will turn
The space round and above
With
All my
Unconditional . . . love.

Jill Barker

TWENTIES

When you are eighty and dying,
what is left from your twenties?
Your skin is rotting you,
your cosmetics are giving you away,
your hairs are greying in silence,
slipping away while you are sleeping.
What is left by then?
My heart never leaves you,
Even one day when you are lying under the green land,
if you return
with just a little,
a little tinge of whisper you make with the wind that sends you here,
even though I am sleeping,
I will love you as the twenties I do.

Thiam Kok Lau

SAY YES!

It isn't just your lovely face
That makes my sluggish pulses race.
It isn't just your saucy smile
That glows, and makes my day worthwhile,
Or cheeky bum and perky breasts
(That, in my thoughts, I dare caress).
It's knowing that you care for me,
Without your love what would I be?
Across the room I catch your eyes,
Exhilarated, mesmerised.
You bring me joy, you make me laugh,
You are my love, my other half.
And you will make my whole world shine
If you will be my valentine.

Liz Rolph

PERHAPS YOU KNOW

Perhaps you know who sends you this,
Who plies you with his artifice,
Who wrote these verses in your card -
To tease your mind and test your heart -
And signed an as yet unknown kiss.

Tossed off into his hopes' abyss,
You must have guessed these lines are *his;*
And what his well-wished words impart,
Perhaps you know . . .

He likes you. That is all there is
As yet. His dreams you may dismiss
(For fictions fail and fall apart).
But could these bare foundations start
An incremental edifice?
Perhaps, you know.

Chris Young

VALENTINE

V   is for valentine
A   is for always
L   is for love
E   is for each of us
N   is for notice you care
T   is for two of us
I   is for irresistible you are
N   is for nice of you to care
E   is for email me
     I love you.

Norma Elaine

TO MY VALENTINE

To my valentine,
A day to spend with the one you love,
Praying, that the lover is sent from above.
Is it just for the day or for many more?
Or will it be like an eagle, soar?

To my valentine,
May this day be more than others celebrate,
Celebrating love with a lifelong mate.
God put us together for a reason:
To let His love pour out forever, and not for a season.

To my valentine,
I love you with all my heart and soul,
If there were no God, in me there would be a hole.
He fills that space with someone like you,
To love and to hold, to be faithful and true.

To my valentine,
No one is luckier in knowing you,
Holding you till a new day breaks through;
Saying, 'Good morning,' to the one I love.
'Good morning', a prayer answered from above.

To my valentine,
So, let every day be a Valentine's Day in our lives,
Understanding and standing by each other's side.
Being one in God and His marvellous love,
He has fitted us together - like a hand in a glove.

Hoosain D Banoo

VALENTINE'S DAY

Tomorrow would be Valentine's
Her heart was all a-flutter
Would the postman bring a card?
What sweet words would it utter?

The postman came, the postman went
And nothing did deliver
With broken heart she went to work
And cried herself a river.

All day she waited by the phone
But still he did not call
How could he forget her
Who loved him most of all.

Came 5 o'clock and home she went
With heavy steps and sad
It was the worst St Valentine's
That she had ever had.

She reached the flat with key in hand
And opened up the door
But still there were no messages
Lying on the floor.

And then she heard soft music
Come from another room
And smelled the scent that only comes
When roses are in bloom.

She looked inside and what she saw
Did her heavy heart relieve
For he had unexpectedly
Been given two weeks leave.

Ian Russell

UNKNOWN

I've watched her now for such a time
I feel I know her well.
No introduction has been made,
In spite of this, I fell.

I fell for her contagious smile
The way she shakes her hair,
The confidence that in her glows,
Her independent air.

The gentle softness in her eyes
That shows compassion waits
For he who captures this sweet heart
And intertwines their fates.

But not for me this thought of love,
Too many years divide
For she is young and sweet and true
These lives will not collide.

So I must now content myself
To keep my feelings low
And thank the stars from which she sprang,
That she will never know.

Franz Grimley

WHAT IS LOVE?

Some ponder that love is friendship
Some believe in love at first sight
Others think that love's for a pet
Or the love in the Heaven's light

Some think that love is beautiful
Some believe they must have it there
Others want each other happy
They use love for kindness and care

Love is the bringer of happiness
Love can be the caring and joy
But love can be used by evil
Controlled like a small child's toy

People are torn by emotions
They blame this mysterious thing
While others believe it's a gift
And they say it conquers all sin

Love can't be want or desire
Nor some kind of mystical need
Love is the power of kindness
It's not for the power of greed.

Samuel Edwards

DRIVEN-PASSION

P rodding. Piercing. Percolating. Pressurising, pyrotechnical passion!
A bsorbing. Alluring. Activating. Adulterating. Animated lustful
   addiction, turning wheels of desire!
S hamelessly seducing, selfishly schooling and sculpting,
   shaping fashion!
S timulating. Sinisterly scheming. Soul-searcher. Sensationally
   secreting an inspirational fire!
I nducing. Indulging. Inspiring. Illuminating. Impassioned, immoral,
   incinerating assassin!
O utlandish occupant, that obscenely obsessive, omnipresent,
   spiritual amplifier!
N on-conforming nemesis, nurturing and nourishing a Driven-Passion.

Michael Hinks

COLOUR OF LOVE

Who and when was it ever said,
That the colour of love is depicted by red?
For true love sees no colour, its shade is neutral -
A colourless chemistry, a feeling that's mutual.
The rush of love, as your eyes meet
The touch of two hands, you can *hear* your heart beat,
Floating on air - as if you have no feet
Two pairs of lips lock . . . and the taste, o' so sweet.
It happens so fast, that you hardly dare breathe
No control of your body, as all sense takes leave.
Exhale slowly, as pulses race,
No need for words, it's written clearly on your face.
In upturned corners of mouth and your pupils dilate,
Could this be him . . . your true soulmate?
The eternal question, answered only by fate.

Sadie Fletcher

OH! BE MY VALENTINE
(Dedicated to my husband, Graeme)

Beneath the dim light I sit,
Curtains drawn,
Soft music soothing the soul,
Candles flickering,
And a glowing fire to warm the room.
I now wait with bated breath.
Bubbly Pongracz chilled on ice.
The dry Brut style just waiting to pop the cork,
Fresh, creamy and a touch of baked apples,
Such aroma all in a sparkling bubble,
So widely praised, just like you
Come on home my valentine,
It is dinner for two,
Tall glass stems to fill with bubbly,
Chin-chin.

Nadine Mackie

THAT'S WHY I LOVE YOU
(Poem dedicated to Margaret McElvenny)

In the darkness of winter
Wet and cold I look at you!
You lift my blues with the warmth of your smile
The buds of spring begin to open
While the birds sing as butterflies spread their wings.
The sun shines from the light blue sky
There is warmth all around
What can this be, is it magic?
No! It's the glow of your aura,
You're beautiful inside and out.
That's why I love you
Please be my valentine.

Duncan MacFarlane

LONELY

My dear,
Please listen to my every word
I write with tears upon this page.
My love is like a lonely bird
Imprisoned in its gilded cage.

My love,
Every day I feel the pain
Of love that I know cannot be
Unless you come to me again.
Only you can set me free.

Sweetheart,
The second month, the fourteenth day
Is etched upon my aching heart.
Oh, that we could chase away
What is keeping us apart.

Lover,
All my thoughts are with you now,
So send me soon a hopeful sign
That you will come to me somehow
And be my loving valentine.

Brian Laidlaw

THE BEST MAN
(To my husband, who is the best of everything to me)

You believed in me from the start
as I believed in you
and together we grew.
I didn't think I would love you
quite as much as I do,
but I do.
You are the best man
for me,
it's true.
Our hearts beat together
to the same rhythm,
in perfect time.
We could be soul twins,
created beyond
this mortal time that we share.
One day will come
when we have to let go
of each other's hand.
And I pray you'll wait for me,
for you will always be
the best man for me.

Gilly Jones

TO MY FIRST AND LAST LOVE

One January you wrote my name in snow
So that the arching sky would know
How much I meant to you.

In March I scratched a cross upon a stone,
Secret between us it was known,
The symbol of our love.

In June in the dry, warm wood we lay
Loving the afternoon away.
As evening dropped its gentle dew,
On our favourite tree a heart you drew
With tiny letters for me and you.

The years have passed,
The snow's long gone,
Rain and moss have smoothed the stone,
But the simple heart has strangely grown
Fuller and softer, like our own.

Barbara Roberts

NO VALENTINE

If a sweetheart I did have,
He'd be more than my valentine,
For no one day is more special,
Than each and every one,
No Mr Right for some of us,
Through varied circumstances,
Still there's love to spread about,
Without a sweetheart in sight,
So to all of us independent ones,
A love of life, and God of course,
To keep us on the happiest course.

Rachel Taylor

INNOCENCE

Plunk of unplugged guitar string and you serenade me,
Concentration on face, I'm wrapped in blankets of ecstasy.
Unvoiced thoughts understood through trembling hand,
Passionate embrace I float to enchanted land.

Candles elongate, tender shadows of raw exhilaration,
Undiscovered feelings pure emotional adoration.
Freedom of expression through intimate discovery,
Reach levels of intensity, you fulfil me completely.

A rush of beautiful emotion and I am left breathless,
Lost in passionate time and trembling helplessness.
Extinguished candles, wrapped in peaceful sleep,
Sweet emotion floats in air, feeling a love so deep.

I wake with arms wrapped tight around me,
We are wrapped in blankets of ecstasy.
Dreams are broken and stir in sleep,
This moment in mind forever shall keep.

Samantha Whitehouse

A PERFECT PAIR

You're like a tube of toothpaste
And I squeeze you every day.
You bring a sparkle to my life
With your kind and loving ways.
The roses that you give me
To let me know you care
Confirms the feeling in my heart
That we're a perfect pair.

Vera M Higginson

AS LONG AS I HAVE YOU
(To Carolyn)

When we have to separate, it's then I fully know
How fervently I care for you - I swoon to see you go!
So many precious days we've spent together 'neath the sun,
I never thought we'd say and do the things we've said and done.
Lazy days of laughter, of passion cake and prawns,
Of holding hands and seagulls, of cut and uncut lawns.
Of babysitting neighbours' kids, of praying and advice,
Of fish and chips and chocolate and other things quite 'nice'.
Of musicals and photographs, of people-watching too,
Of evening meals alfresco and whisp'ring, 'I love you.'

You are a dream I'm living in, too perfect to be real.
A thousand words could never tell the way you make me feel.
Already I am aching, once again, for your embrace
But every time I close my eyes I see your lovely face.
One glance at that sweet countenance - my cares all disappear,
My heart becomes a singing bird whenever you are near.
I soar like summer swallows who've never felt so high
And like the vapour trails of planes, leave patterns in the sky.

Though undeserving, I have won a prize beyond compare:
The closest of companions, as astute as you are fair.
Could we lay upon the pebbles of a quiet shore,
And, holding one another, stay like that for evermore
When tears rush in, as do the tides, we'll be all right you'll see,
As long as I have you, my dear, and you, my dear, have me.

Matthew Pickhaver

STRONGER

Can't you see the pain that I'm going through,
Is it 'cause I'm blonde or no good for you?
Is it 'cause we're friends and nothing else?
I can't just put my feelings for you on the shelf.
Everything about you is so very sweet
And even when you smile I drop at your feet.
I will keep you warm when you are cool,
I know that when I'm around you that I act the fool.

You make me stronger
And you make me smile
And sometimes when I'm lonely,
I think of you for a while.
So let me know how you're feeling,
Don't keep it in let me know,
That you're feeling happy
And if you want to I will go.

Sometimes I think together we'd be really great,
I'll never let you down; I'll never be late.
I'll treat you like the way you deserve to be,
I'll make you feel you're wanted, I'll make you feel free.
I may not have much money, the car, or the looks,
So what if I like my music, my films and my books.
And when you're down I will pick you up,
Then I will put some tea in your coffee cup.

Lawrence Hollett

THE SLINGS AND ARROWS OF OUTRAGEOUS CUPID

When I first saw Cupid, I thought, *How irresponsible*
To let a child of that age play with a bow and arrow!
Someone might get hurt. Just then, the little sod
Pinged an arrow off his bow and skewered me
To a most unsuitable boy.
He looked young enough to be my little brother.

The boy took me for a thrill ride,
On his motorbike, down an almost vertical hill.
At the top I thought, *I am going to die!*
By the time we hit the bottom I *had* almost died.
I had almost died of laughter.

The boy took me for a spin in his car.
I had to climb in through the window,
Because the door wouldn't open.
He pushed the car down the hill, until the engine
Woke up screaming in terror at the gradient,
While we screamed with laughter.

The boy's house was so cold that we went to bed
In woollies. We laughed our socks off
And the rest of our clothes followed.
A baby was born. That wiped the smile off my face
For a bit. Then the baby opened his eyes, and ours,
And we laughed till we cried tears of joy.

When I woke up this morning I could not see the boy,
In his place was a man my own age.
Then he laughed.
Had the boy grown older? Or had I grown younger?
I don't know. But I do know one thing.
Cupid had the last laugh after all.

Kerry-Ann Fender

LOVE LIKE AN ORCHID

Seductive words won't slide him
Into submission
He's too level-headed!
Carefully chosen compliments
Won't convince
He plays them down!

He doesn't see
The great value he holds for me.

He just knows
I appreciate him.
He understands
I treasure him.
He accepts
My love for him.

His kindness always surprises me.
His patience seems limitless.
Practicality romance's rival at times
Dripping red roses
Not an expression of his heart!

A flower may touch you -
For the beauty it holds
May be reminiscent
Of a passion for the natural
And an echo of
The beauty of
The love I have for you.

Then I shall bring an orchid
On Valentine's Day.

Lorraine Burden

A TOAST TO LOVE!

Love can blossom for any age,
The teenage Romeo, the elderly sage!
Love is a teasing, love is a pleasing,
A seasoning of love a delight.

The bouquet of a vintage wine,
The sparkle of champagne,
The scent of stocks at eventide, or roses after rain,
To all these compounds, add the melody of a violin,
And love walks in!

Who can measure all that pleasure
All those hopes, desires and tears,
All that laughter, all that humour?
Love's healing power dispels our fears.

Love disentangles ragged nerves and seeks to soothe and smooth
To give, caress and give again, is what love most aspires
Love's an inextinguishable flame,
Bright kindling of heart's desires . . .

Beryl Moorehead

A CHAIN OF CRANES
(Dedicated to Abbey Lee)

A chain of cranes with a dying heart
Made in bitter tears for the one I love
Who no longer wants to love me back.

As life goes on and time draws by
My love remains with my loneliness
Love has no happiness, love has no joy.

Paul Chan

MY VALENTINE

(For Sasha)

Hold my heart gently, dear lover of mine,
As you sit with me quietly, with limbs all entwined.
With your sweet tiny nose and your cute little face,
You've bewitched me by charm, by your scent, by your grace.

I was tired out from crying salt-drying tears,
I've not loved like this for too many years.
My life was in tatters, I'd fallen apart,
One look - and you'd captured my splintered, fine heart.

As you cuddle up close and cat-like you purr,
I'm seduced just to sit here, stroking your fur.
One look - and I knew it - right from the start,
Just remember, my darling, your paws hold my heart!

Anita Richards

MUM

(To my dearly beloved loving mum)

You are all you seem to be,
The sunshine at daybreak,
The star shine at night,
I look up to Heaven above, the horizon,
I am blessed you're mine . . .

Who has a heart that's true?
Who has that magic touch?
Who is it that means so much and knows what to say?
And that's why I am wishing you
Happy Valentine's Day!

Matthew Willbye

THIS LOVE

Let me die in your arms
It would be so bitter-sweet
And love me with your charms
With all your being greet

Sit me as a child
On your lap surround
Lift me up on high
Hush me with your sound

Oh what is this love
I have known so well?
Many cannot know
Many cannot tell

You have felt the hurt
From unintended pain
But your love for me
Will never be in vain

For I will love you
Till the end of time
Talk to your quiet heart
With my simple rhyme

If this life is all there is
I will gladly be content
And if there is no eternity
Then this is my Heaven-sent

Hold me in your arms
Hold me in your dreams
See me in your future
This love is all it seems

And when tomorrow comes
And when tomorrow goes
We can say that this love
Has no enemies or foes

This love runs so deep
Many chasms it can hold
This love is undying
This love may not be bought or sold.

Peter Ellis

JANET'S POEM

Give me your arms
I will give you my arms
Give me your softness
I will give you my strength
Give me your hope
I will give you mine
Give me your care
I will give you the same
Give me your warmth
I will keep you warm
Give me your heart
All my heart is yours
Give me your love
I will give my love
Give me your soul
I will give you mine
Give me your all
I will give you me.

Ian Cresswell

A VALENTINE PUZZLE
(Alan my husband and valentine)

What makes a valentine?
That's something I can't say
But I know he is mine forever and a day.

How did it happen, what did I miss
Was it something in his eyes
Perhaps it was his kiss?
I would only know if I was very wise.

It's not something that is found in a book
What did he see in me
Not just that I can cook
Is it to do with my company?

Is it a puzzle only known to God above
Or a basic part of life
That makes two strangers fall in love
And then become man and wife?

It doesn't really matter, the how and the why.
I just know he's the best in all the earth and sky
There is no more to say
But he will be my valentine forever and a day!

Angela Robinson

To My DIY Valentine

I put you on a pedestal
Or rather up a ladder
My valentine, my handyman,
I couldn't have been gladder.
But as the years come and go
Although you're still appealing
I wish you'd get your finger out
And finish off the ceiling.

The plaster's old (like us) and cracked
The paint has started peeling
And now you've put the coving up,
You say it still needs sealing.
You'll have to fill in all the cracks
Apply two coats of paint
An undercoat and overcoat
The chance seems somewhat faint
That you'll be done by Easter
Or Christmas two-o-five
But could you try to get it done
While we are both alive!

Mary Hodges

TO YOU I GIVE
(Dedicated to the one I love)

To you I give my loving words,
To cherish and to hold.
To show you how much you are loved,
With words so true and bold.

To you I give my arms to hold,
To keep you safe and warm.
So you will never feel the pain,
That once had left you torn.

To you I give my truth and trust,
On me you can depend.
Together we will face the world,
Until the very end.

To you I give you all I have,
My dreams, my hopes, my fears.
My past, my now, my things to come
And all that I hold dear.

Melanie Cook

VALENTINE'S CARD FOR CHARLIE DIMMOCK

Romantics chose
Charlie Dimmock
Laughter like open lilies
Scent attracts a million sightseers,
Her smile brings flowers to open on a Valentine's Day
Her red hair brings florists to flourish.

Alan Hattersley

THANK YOU KAREN

I'd die if we did part,
I love you with all my heart,
It fills me with such emotion,
My love is as deep as the ocean,
More and more each day,
I love you more than words can say,
You help me face my fears
And wipe away my tears,
I'm glad you light up my life,
Thank you for being my wife,
You are my lover and my friend,
My love for you will never end,
You are the apple of my eye
And will always be until I die,
You're like an angel from Heaven above,
Thank you Karen, with all my love.

Ian White

IF LOVE

If love could make a dream
And dreams could come true
Then darling I'd fall straight in love with you
If I could make a promise
And you could trust my heart
I'd stand right by your side from the start
Can you roll sevens or elevens
Or is life going to be snake eyes?
Can you still know what I'm thinking
Or is it all a surprise?
Every time I see you I see something new
Either in your golden hair or your eyes so blue
Nothing can change the way I feel about you.

Andrew Goldstraw

THE MERMAID'S SONG

In an unseen bay, down by the sea
Rest the hearts of my true love and me
Once together, now parted are we
By sudden death
No longer breathes she

In a high old city, far from the sea
Where air is befoul'd and no one at ease
I struggled and tired from day to day
Unlike myself
In so many ways

In a barnacl'd city, very deep in the sea
There was a young mermaid dreaming of me
And from Neptune's lagoon to the coral reef fayres
Together we swam
Seven oceans to share

Then in ruined Atlantis, far under the sea
This young mermaid did whisper to me,
'One day I will find you, alone in a bay.'
Months went by, waiting
Until came that day

In an unseen bay, down by the sea
I had to bury my mermaid, my dream
For she swam here to me and yet was sick
From a blight, a poison
A man-made oil slick

In an unseen bay, down by the sea
Rest the hearts of my true love and me
Once together, now parted are we
By sudden death
No longer breathes she.

Gregory James

THIS LOVE

Though my art is in words
yet I have none to speak my love for you.
Love such as this
will not be bound in rhyme or metre
nor confined in artful verse.
With such love as this
no heart ever before stirred
nor words ever captured
nor song ever celebrated such love.

But still my heart will not be silenced.
For in you I have found my solace
and my soul's companion.
In you my heart has discovered
its breadth and its heights.
In you I have found my keystone,
and the fit is perfect,
and makes sense of everything,
and there are no mysteries left
save that we should question or try to explain.

Wait not on tomorrow
for in this moment lies all our tomorrows,
and dwell not on yesterday
for all our yesterdays were but
a preparation for this moment.
And there is no improving on this moment
for there is no improving on this love.

Gwyn Winter

BOY MEETS GIRL
(Almost)

Under the clock they said they'd meet,
His hands were blue,
He stamped his feet.
She didn't sound the sort of girl to let a fella down,
They decided on the phone last night to have some fun in town.
Said she knew the clock in question (7.30 was her suggestion)
Time went by and still he stood, his feet now felt like blocks of wood.
I'll wait, he thought, *till half-past eight, and then find myself*
another date.

On the other side of town, his date stood with a puzzled frown.
The clock he'd said, without a doubt,
Looked as if he'd blown her out
As she waited, time to think,
Last night she'd been just on the brink
She'd leave her partner, let him see, how independent she could be . . .
How dare he treat her in this way?
She'd soon show him. Make him pay.
Arrange a blind date, have a fling, give her life a bit of zing!

How much longer shall she wait, or is this the hand of fate?
Last night's anger starts to cool,
Maybe I've just been a fool . . .
I'll go back, start again,
Life's too short for all this pain!
Two lessons here for life's great file . . .
Step back from anger for a while
And always check the clock!

Betty Holman

VALENTINE INVENTORY

I want to buy you
Roses, crisp,
Pink, passionate,
Red, linen,
White.
I want to buy you
Chocolates, rich
Superior, Belgian,
Or possibly
Turkish delight.
I want to buy you
Wine, expensive,
Chilled, Chardonnay,
With two glasses
To drink at night.
I want to write you
Poems, valentines
Sonnets, soliloquy,
Villanelle, romantic,
Not trite.

I want to give you my
Everything, my world,
My universe,
Myself,
My heart

My life.

Janet M Baird

SWEET VALENTINE
(Dedicated to Ian Bowes)

Take a moment from your life to love me
Hold me for a heartbeat in your thoughts
Draw me near as you sleep at night
Kiss my lips by dawn's breaking light
Dream I lay beside you, valentine

Take a second from your day to want me
To whisper all the things I long to hear
Send each word upon a prayer
So I can worship without care
At the altar of my desire, valentine

Take a moment from your life to love me
Allow your mind to linger now and then
While the moonbeams from above
Build a staircase with my love
That will lead you to my heart, sweet valentine.

Elizabeth Bowes

WATER FLOWS

I have touched your soul
Come into the quiet place
You have seduced my heart
Aroused my inner being
We merge; our passions fuse
All our senses are united
In a love that seems eternal

But water flows . . .

Tanya Roddie

WITH APOLOGIES TO WILL SHAKESPEARE - TO MY VALENTINE

Let not the marriage of true minds
Admit that romance has not mellowed through time,
Love is not love if it changes not in kind.
Our moods adapt from mundane to sublime.
Your sense of humour and the twinkling eyes
Still make me laugh and remind me of youth
And life moves on from low to high,
It's never dull with you, forsooth.
Your hair's gone grey, your distinguished mouth
Is replicated by the sound of your drill's sweet voice.
But time has gone, we see future's growth
And joy and sorrow helps us rejoice.
My love for you has deepened yet
In time fulfilled with no regret.

Gael Nash

CHIVALRY

Love from afar is love in purest kind,
That asks for naught, and naught gets in return.
That, in refusal, truthfulness can find
And thrills to hear a voice, though that voice spurns.
Love is not love, that seeks to get some gain,
For lovers seek to give and not to take.
'For thee' is every loving heart's refrain,
That seeks to act for someone else's sake.
No true love ever made selfish demand,
Or acted for the sake of feeling good,
Nor strove to steal away another's hand,
But merely offered all for which they stood.
Love from afar is love in purest wise,
That lies not on the lips, but in the eyes.

Gavin Steele

MARGAUX'S VALENTINE PLEA

(From Margaux, aged one year, waiting for a heart transplant, to the mother of a child who is about to die)

Valentine's Day and all I want is a heart.
Not the chocolate kind, foil-wrapped
with truffle core, but beating
just beyond death.

I cannot eat and barely drink, and when I do,
a single suck triggers sweaty panic,
my fingers cool from the tip
and my heart staggers and stops.

Then I grow cold, still as a wax doll,
life just beyond my fingers' grasp,
only Maman's cry pulls me back,
'Je suis désolé Margaux, désolé, désolé, désolé.'

Her face is tortured, her love on the rack,
with sorrow no one can know,
her eyes brimful drop tears
so warm my heart will overflow.

Though my flesh was torn and sewn and torn and sewn again,
my heart is beyond repair,
but I live for her as she lives for me,
on this see-saw of hope and despair.

I need a heart to see tomorrow,
my chance for life hangs on a death,
the death of a child, so cherished, like yours,
slipping away in your arms.

You could be the one who decides
whether my dwindling life survives.
Two babies, two mothers, two agonies,
one heart.

So will it be two deaths or one?

Katrina Bride

BUTTERFLY TATTOO

Do you remember
This time last year?
We went to London
And bought tickets for the theatre.
You wore your tarnished silver watch
That I'd given you for your birthday.
But even though,
We were still late.

Do you remember
Feeding the geese and swans
And how I hadn't smiled in so long?
You made me so happy that day,
Just for being you -
And oh how you laughed
When I said I wanted a butterfly tattoo.

Do you remember
Passing by the London Eye?
An old lady sitting by herself,
Weeping a drunken smile.
How it made me sad
To see someone so alone,
But you said it wasn't so bad,
She's remembering a love still strong.

I'll always remember
This time last year.
You were the angel
That gave me the truth of friendship.
So here's to you this year,
Eleanor, I love you still,
Happy valentine, my beautiful angel.

Dan Laurie

MISSING YOU

Days went faster than I could say,
Our love silently went away,
These empty years without your touch
And your gentle smile I've missed so much,
Only a photograph of your face,
But in my heart there's an empty space,
I pray for you to come along to fill that empty space
And make my heart strong
When I think of you I shed a tear,
Hoping that you'll soon be near,
We found love I won't forget
And the love we found I won't regret,
Violet all my love for Valentine's Day
Wish you were with me for Valentine's Day.

Ernest Stokes

FOR MICHAEL

Love is like a flower
Love is like a tree
Love is like that red, red rose
Blooming just for me
Love is like sweet music
Cascading from a harp
Love is like the song
Of a nightingale or lark
All sweet poetic phrases
All of them are true
How much sweeter . . .
How much simpler . . .
Love is . . . me and you!

Marji Tomlinson

LOVE WITHOUT LABELS

After many months of filing
Explaining, typing down
I thought I'd got it sorted
Every detail known.
A completely foolproof structure
Neatly stored on disc
Computer complex programme
Nothing had been missed.

Then you walk in up the stairs
Systems suddenly crash
E-mails spin in virtual space
Deleted, sent to trash.
When I thought I knew it all
I'd missed one crucial part
Real love can't be filed away
In folders labelled 'heart'.

Mano Warren

ALWAYS MY VALENTINE

Always my valentine
You will always be my valentine
Mine is an immortal love
A feeling so intense
Understand?
It will never make sense
Desire so strong
Does it have to be wrong?
Tell me, are you lonely?
Do you feel as alone as me?

Victoria Golding

LIKE A ROSEBUD

*(I dedicate this poem to my husband David. This is to say thank you for being by my side,
throughout all we have been through in the last few years)*

Like a rosebud,
my love for you has grown,
when we first met, my emotions I could never show,
with your patience and understanding,
I began to open up,
like the petals of a rosebud in bloom.
New possibilities have come my way,
it feels like the sun has finally shone on me,
the darkness has gone away,
like a rose in flower on a summer's day.
You make me laugh so much,
each and every day,
we are on this road together,
finding our way.
Old petals may fall off this red rose flower,
but new petals grow,
just like new experiences coming our way.
The most important thing of all,
like a gardener caring for his precious rose,
I care for you deeply and love you very much
and I always will.

Emma Jane Lambert

THE YEAR

In February she came awake,
Saw him move with athletic grace.
He let her into his mind, his soul,
Haunted by her fragile face.

In summer, she felt his gentle touch,
A protective embrace beneath the trees.
Her trust, a precious gift to him,
A wood nymph lying amongst the leaves.

In autumn, passion she'd never known,
His love a certainty, like death.
A woman now within his arms,
Growing bolder with every breath.

In winter, her lover tender and strong,
She knows his thoughts for they're her own.
He knows that he can never leave,
She's deep within his blood, his bone.

In February, they make a promise,
To stay together for all time.
Two stars in the midnight blue,
Her secret, his secret valentine.

Samantha Philo-Gill

AFTER THE STORM . . . (A FORBIDDEN LOVE)

If I was a cupid, oh where would I prance,
As I see him he sees her and together they dance.
Gently he whispers from his lips to her ear,
As the moonlight shines boldly upon her red hair.
He speaks of her beauty with an uncontrolled smile,
He admires her softness with elegance and style.
He needs no response as he looks into her eyes,
He cradles her warmth as the passion undies.

They descend from the balcony to where the autumn leaves lay,
His hand on her heart, a secret she did pray.
To my Lord up above with this hand on my heart,
Please grant me one wish, that my true love never part.
As he gently uplifts her porcelain face,
No lies, no deception for there is no trace.
She confides of her secret of which she had sent,
Of her undying love even death could not end.

He deeply dives into the pools of her eyes,
A tear trickled gently, no maybe a cry.
This tear is for happiness of my love at its peak,
For you are the one of my love I do speak.
I looked down upon them as they held on so tight,
There was a glow of their love as one in the night.
I floated down calmly with grace and divine,
Her wish I did grant as their lips intertwined.

Their moment must end as the moonlight does fade,
But now they can go on with the strength that they gave.
As he watches her dance through the enchanted trees,
Her gown was flowing with the games of the breeze.
While he is on the steps to Heaven does stare,
Thanking this night for the power to dare.

How can this be . . . ?
For I am the cupid to deliver 'God's' touch,
My journey unknown and power as much.
My arrow was poised, but alas I did wait,
For their love as written on His eternal gate.

Lee Mak

A VALENTINE'S KISS

You told me I was beautiful the night we first met
Your Prince Charming-like advances, were ones I couldn't reject.
We indulged in some rather intriguing conversation
To receive a valentine's kiss was one of my expectations.

So a solemn sign of affection was what I was looking to show
A single red rose I gave to you and a sexy smile made me glow.
You then touched me on the hand and that gave me a clue
A valentine's kiss from you to me was long overdue.

I felt like a princess in my fuschia pink and white dress
The silent gesture with your eyes told me you didn't want to suppress.
To take me in your arms was what I had dreamt for
A passionate valentine's kiss was all I wanted, I couldn't ask for
anything more.

I was flurried with nerves, as you drove me home
The soft beat of the music and my heartbeat, alone.
To take my hand again and to make all my wishes come true
A valentine's kiss clearly told me how much I was in love with you.

Frances Morrison

HE SAID THREE WORDS

(For Rodger . . . may my ears always hear you say those three words and my mouth always reply)

He said three words and captured me
Who once thought love a fantasy
A dream, a hope, devised by fools
Or simply just a worn out tool

His words they took me by surprise
It's hard for me to realise
How through these scars he beauty sees
Or why he wanted, needed, me

He said three words in whispered breaths
And somehow touched my inner depths
How could I answer, mute reply
And still he waited, softly sighed

I've used up all my foolish whims
What have I left to offer him?
A tattered heart whose lame disguise
Would fool not even blind man's eyes

He said three words, they fell on ears
That craved that sound for countless years
Betrayed by tongue, with tear-filled eyes
I answered back in warm reply.

Ruth Kephart

PLEASE CHANGE THE HABIT OF A LIFETIME
(To my wonderful husband, Murray. Let's make our life together even lovelier)

You've never been my valentine.
Forty-four years together and yet,
Never a card or a bunch of flowers
On this special day. Not from the outset.

I know you love me. You tell me often
And demonstrate it in many diverse ways.
But, unlike most lovers, you won't display
Your love on the most romantic of days.

It's that infuriating stubborn streak again.
You've never liked direction or control:
'No one's telling me when to say I love you.'
I appreciate the sentiment, but that does not console.

Our half century is fast approaching.
True love deepens with each year.
Please change the habit of a lifetime,
And be a valentine to this old dear.

Valerie Catterall

SOULMATE - LOST

I miss
your reading an
unwritten book; the touch
of your looks unweaving my grief.
Aching.

John Winfield

TRIBUTE
(To Trish from George)

If there were endless days in which to show my love
'twould need the help of angels from above
to sing your praises loud and clear,
the reasons why I hold you, my love, so dear.

If all the stars fell from the sky,
I, for one, would not question, why?
For it would be part of my dream
to enshrine your glorious features' gleam
of brilliance the whole wide world to light;
never would the Earth have been more bright.

Yet must this adoration meet untimely death
then no longer would I wish for breath
to keep me alive when you are gone
for without your presence misery has begun.

Thora Beddard

WOW

I'm attracted to you like a moth to a flame,
I jump when I hear your name!
With you I'm like a child on Christmas Day!
Say you'll never go away!
Let's stay together for evermore!
As you're the one I really adore.
Let's be together, happy and bright,
Right up until God says goodnight!

Gwynfa Evans

THE RED ROSE (OWEN)

The tall, straight stem,
Your strong, upstanding form,
Wide, green leaves,
The surrounding love you give.
Sharp, thick barbs,
Your emotional protection,
Soft, red petals,
Your caring sharing ways.
That enhanced calming fragrance,
Your gentle, consuming touch.
Bold, red colour,
Your courageousness and strength.
That beautiful red rose,
Depicts our perfect match!

I love you!

Jennifer Collins

LOOK INTO YOU HEART

P oems are in our hearts, it's the way that we all feel.
O ur feelings become verses, and then that makes them real.
E very day that passes is full of mystery and rhyme.
T hese things we should write about, if only we had time.
R oses lose their petals, and then they fade away.
Y our feelings become poems and then they're here to stay.

Barbara Russell

AFFECTIONATELY, A MESSAGE TO MY SWEET LOVE

You know, sweet love, I think of you each single waking hour.
And then in sleep, I dream of you, your presence and your power.
Well I think of you when you're not here but when you are I glower,
For such is love destroyed, neglected, left to rot and sour.

Now my love, I hate you more than words can ever say,
If you were here, I'd scream at you to make you go away.
But when you'd gone, I'd smile and think of happier times ago,
When you and I were lovers and not seething, death-sworn foe.

So still it pleases me to hear that you are happy too,
(Although straight in your face I'd spit for all my love for you).
And if you see me on the street you'd better 'walk on by'
('Cause I'm going to try to stamp a cigarette butt in your eye).

But oh sweet love, I'll dream of you and ever wish you here,
Beside me while I sleep or softly whispering in my ear.
For all the hate I feel for you, my bitter enemy,
Was once pure love and so it shall remain eternally.

Oh love, my love, my hate, my foe, I admit to you it calms,
Remembering how once I lay so sweetly in your arms.
And truly could I choose, we would have died right there that day
(But forgetting my revolver, you sadly got away).

And rest assured, I wish you well, my beloved, handsome knave
(For sure you'll do no better until flung into your grave).
And remember if you need a friend in time of grief or doubt,
I'm always looking out for you and waiting, so watch out.

Joanne Madders

It's Written In Our Connection

It's written in the stars
It's for you and me
I saw you walk
Walk past me
I stood there alone
Thinking, wishing you were mine
The love I have
It's written for you
I feel we may have
Have a connection
I see your smile
I see your eyes
I see it's written for you and I
I always wonder
Wonder what it would be like
Like if your life was here
Here with me
I wish your love could take
Take my hands into yours
My heart in yours
Am happy it's now written
Written in the stars
Written in our connection
I now know it's written
For you, I wish you could see.

Angela Cole

DANCE OF A LIFETIME

I met you at the St Valentine's dance,
you wore a glittering ballroom gown,
which matched the colour of your eyes,
you looked the most beautiful girl in town,
heart-shaped balloons of all colours and size
above our heads were hung,
couples were waltzing around the room
whilst 'I'll be your sweetheart' was sung,
everybody was happy, they were all having fun,
and St Valentine knew, that hearts were being won,
by the giving of a red rose,
to someone for whom they cared
and a card adorned with kisses
meant romance was in the air.
There's been many an engagement
announced on Valentine's Day,
rings are given, promises made, looks like sunshine all the way,
February fourteenth, we're halfway through the month,
days start to lengthen, and trees begin to sprout,
our romance flourished in the spring
and was soon to be in full bloom.
We planned a life together 'neath the bright light of the moon,
St Valentine we thank you, for your matchmaking success,
for now, my wife like me, is now grown old,
to me, she's still the girl in that beautiful dress.
We are still devoted to each other, come what may,
and we pray that we'll come face to face
with St Valentine, one day.

May Dabrowiecki

TEMPLE OF MY HEART
(To HK)

Is the temple of my heart all secret alcoves, pierced screens
Carved by blind craftsmen,
Their heads filled with the chant of the name of God?

Does the temple of my heart look like a fortress on a high hill,
Unassailable by all, except
Those who know the hidden footways
Bounded by rushing water through the desert?

Are the gardens in the temple of my heart full of roses and jasmine,
Where peace means a still pool reflecting the sky
And humble birds flock in the steadfast pines?

In the temple of my heart do I find you, contemplating
Gold and black fish beneath the water lilies
Waiting for me to invite you in?

Through the temple of my heart,
Do I think you already know the way?

There are no locks to the inner sanctums,
Simply the key to yourself.

See you there.

Pey Colborne

THE FIRELIGHT OF LOVE

Loveliness . . .
In realms of angel,
pure and fair,
fills my stolen heart.
For lips that smile as they do,
and kiss the words that speak,
. . . yet eyes that did awaken
suffering deep
. . . then held me in their fond embrace.
From mind to mind
'cross bound'ries far,
that do not hold,
. . . I gave myself to thee.
With flecks of grey,
that flit and lance . . .
In candlelight . . .
The fairy dance . . .
The firelight . . .
Of love.

Bob Tose

YOUNG LOVE

Let's make this
Valentine's Day special.
Our sights are set
On each other.
We've made everybody cry.

Young love is out
Of the world, because
Nobody understands it.
But, that's not our
Fault.

Kirk Antony Watson

VALENTINE'S POEM

To be a valentine is great, how would I know?
I'm too old now to get a date, how would I know?
Just a card asking me out
Would make me want to scream and shout
Would make me feel a million dollars
Not something out of the house of horrors
I'm not as young as I used to be
But let's be honest, neither is he
I've suffered the ravages of old father time
But I still think I'm in my prime
At 60 something I don't feel old
My hair's not silver, it's a lovely gold
My fingers are long, my figure's trim
Please someone say, god, where have you been?
But fantasy I'm afraid all this
I'll be content to get a kiss.

Jackie Davies

LOVE IS . . .
(For my darling Chris. Always, Amanda)

The gentlest of hearts
The loveliest of smiles
The most beautiful of minds

Softly

They grow

The smoothest of touches
The most colourful eye

Love is you.

Amanda Richards

ODE TO ROBBIE BURNS

(From an Essex girl)

Robbie Burns, you are to me a complete and utter mystery.

Your gorgeous language leaves me tingling
Your metaphors set my toes a jingling
Could I set your heart on fire
If I skelpit thro' the dub and mire?
Would your passion levels rise
If you saw the scaddit in my eyes?

And if you dangled first upon my swee
If I rugged and chugged, would you love me?
And quite beside my muckle troke
You're such a spurtle shankit bloke
Your gawsy luggies are legendary,
Your winnock-bunker, not necessary

My groaning trencher there you fill
Your massive hurdies move me still
I'd like to coost my duddies to the waark
Fling on your crummock in the dark
And if up my lum I vanished sweetly
And my weel-hain'd kebbuck fell down neatly
Would you blether my shoogly knees
In your haffet squattle? Ooh, yes please . . .

Oh Robbie, while you're bousing at the nappy,
Do you think I'd make you happy?
I think if I pronounced it better
And studied word and form and letter
If I had my wishes, they'd surely be
To understand this literacy.

Michele Amos

VALENTINE BE MINE

Allan be mine
I love you with all my heart
I have waited all my life for you
Then five years ago
You came into my life
It was love at first sight
We became a couple
Throughout my life
I had trouble
A failed marriage
Divorced and alone
Two children to consider
But then you came into my life
You took us all on as your own
Never once complained if it got hard
Life's for sharing with the three of us
You shared yourself with us
No children could want for better
Since you came into their life
We have gone from strength to strength
A love that will last the length of time
I am sure this time
The love I feel for this man
Will last forever, my valentine
Now we're getting married
We shall be a family
Everyone is happy
Valentine's Day so special
For all four of us forever a family.

Janet Hopkins

THE POSTMAN STOLE MY VALENTINE

The postman stole my valentine, the one you sent to me
Sealed with all your pretty kisses so romantically
Just like me you see he wishes you were his girlfriend
And he's jealous so he intercepts, all of the love you send

The postman stole my valentine, it was him now I can tell
Cos you know that Christmas card you sent, he took that as well
Along with the note you wrote to say thanks when I promised
                                                    you the moon
And even those passionate love letters, scented with your perfume

But I should not hold him to blame, surely I would do the same
I know I would not feel ashamed to steal you all for myself
Here in this heart of mine I don't think it would be a crime
And if you were my valentine, I'd never ever share you
                                                    with anyone else

The postman stole my valentine; well you see he must have done
How else could a man as handsome as me not even receive one?
There's lots of girls who like me and it's beyond all belief
There's no other explanation, the postman must be a thief.

Mark Handley

LOVE'S WAY

A walk in the dark, a kiss in the park, two lovers meet.
A flickering light, a park bench at night, two lovers cuddle.
That magic they share with romance in the air dazzled by
                                                    the moon that night.
With stars in their eyes they both realise that their hearts belong
                                                    to each other.

R Morgan

MY GREATEST REWARD

I have sown and I have reaped,
Did all I could to achieve greatness
I have fought and won the battles
Sang all the verses of the septet
I have gone and I have come
Overtaking every obstacle near and far
I have studied and now a-learned
Conquered every goblin on my way,
But here is a deep reservoir of love that is empty
Who shall fill it up?
I am like a debutante on her first outing
Searching for love in my heart
My reservoir needs to be filled
Who shall be my reward?
I am under the sedation of love
As I sing my serenade
Now that you have come
With a paean of love
I went into rhapsody over the love you showed me
The parody of my love
Now listen to my greatest reward,
I have a rumba in my heart
Even the Indians cannot beat my calypso
I capitulate to the stand of your love
Your love so strong and tall
It has driven me scatty
Could this ever be my reward?
Yes I know, your love is my greatest reward.

Seun Ogunbajo

DATE WITH A DISH

Valentine

Sensual,
Delight
Like wine and coffee

Quality
Is complex
Of good
Beans, fully roasted
Semi-sweet and bitter-sweet
Just like
The coverture.

This treat
Will give you
Chocolate sensations
That will
Satisfy
Your cravings.

A reason
To celebrate
Valentine's Day
One of the simple
Pleasures of life.

Alexander Osunwoke

IF YOU . . .

If you loved me
For a day
Would my sorrow
Fade away?

If you loved me
For a week
Would I reach
My highest peak?

If you loved me
For a month
Or so
Would I never feel low?

If you loved me
For a year
Would my heartache
Just disappear?

If you loved me
For all time
In Heaven
Would you still be mine?

Simon McAlear

HE'S

He's fun,
Such fun, that smile, wicked smile,

He's cute,
We suit, together thoughts incline,

He's fast,
Too fast, please make it last,

He's alive,
So alive, moving quickly past

My barriers, breaking them down,
Crumbling all around,

Heart churning, passions burning,
Stop turning,

Let me get off,
I'm not ready for this, but can't resist

So I stay on for the ride,
For maybe, just a while, but,

He's dangerous,
Not quite sure,
Trust, only a word, or a knock at the door

So I pay the price and don't think twice,
It's too good, it's too nice

All those years of guys who didn't measure,
Is this the one I'll treasure,
Forever

The comfortable, closeness notion
Of complete, whole pure emotion,

When I look at him,
Just look at him and sigh

He's - my guy

Hilary Walker

MY VALENTINE

Though springtime flush of youth has passed,
long gone the day we met.
Young love blossomed oh so fast,
strong and deep did get.
Petals of love unfurled that day,
a wonderful moment in time.
Eyes locked together as if to say,
'Please be my valentine'.
Summer came in a golden haze,
snows of winter drifted by.
Together we shared those carefree days,
love soared as high as the sky.
And on a very special day
we became man and wife.
Sharing our hopes along the way,
love living on through life.
Now golden leaves of autumn fall.
Love has mellowed like sweet wine.
Down Memory Lane once again to walk
with my dear valentine.

Josie Rawson

A VALENTINE'S MESSAGE

Hoping that you will have a wonderful day
I cannot be with you, so sorry to say
As we live so very much apart
Of course, you will be there, within my heart

My valentine, my valentine, is what you are
Just like the shining bright star
My thoughts are with you, and when I dream
Dreaming of my love for you, just like a theme

Just like the wings, of a little white dove
That brings the message, so full of love
With a repeated quiet voice, a soft syllable
Now these verses, that are written, says it all

So have a lovely time, on this day of Valentine
Hoping by now, that you know you are mine
Hoping these words are so clear to you, my dear
Perhaps, we shall be together, this time next year.

Jean P McGovern

VALENTINE HEART

My heart is filled with valentine wishes to the lady I did marry.
To look at you when I see you is to make me feel alive,
And to see you smile is to freshen up my heart.
We have our life and we have our future,
We see the stars and the sunrises,
We have our good times, we have our bad,
But we will always have our one true valentine.

Richard G Rust

I LOVE YOU

I love you because you saved me.
I love you because I was falling
And you caught me.
Don't drop me.
Carry me away with you to that place
That I love to be.
I never imagined that I would be
In your arms.
Your everlasting arms.
You see, I love you because you saved me.
I love you because when I called you
You came to me.
When I was drowning
You were my lifeguard, my lifeboat, my float
My front, back and breast stroke
My hair, whilst I play you a melody.
With my whole life in front of me
I want to spend every breath with you.

PS I love you.

Luba Blay-Miezah

ANNE

Take my hand and lead me there
Control my senses all laid bare
Why do I love? Why do I care?
Because you to me are a breath of fresh air

Terence Payne

BLESSED BY GOD
(Dedicated to Mrs Joyce Healy, my wife and lover)

Joyce, I have you in my fortress
And I will never let you depart,
But put you in the dungeons -
In the round, round tower in my heart,
And there,
I will keep you,
Forever,
Yes!
Forever and a day,
Till the walls of my heart,
Crumble,
And my body in dust,
Blows away.
Joyce, I'll love you forever,
On this Earth and in Heaven above,
When we two, unite as angels of love,
You and I,
In a marriage of true love,
Blessed by God, in Heaven above.

The Warrior Poet

TO MY VALENTINE OF FORTY PLUS YEARS (MY WIFE)

You
I looked into those eyes
and they stared back at me,
I was captivated by
what I so hoped would be.

And like starry summer skies
those pretty 'baby-blues',
attracted me to something
I didn't want to lose.

Everything that was in me
lost all of its control,
as I melted down before
those 'windows' to the soul.

The years have only proven
that what I thought was true
and I'm still mesmerised by
those starry eyes of blue.

James A Osteen Jr

MY FAVOURITE

You are my favourite place to be,
Under the sun and next to the sea
Holding you close, close to me,
You are my favourite place to be.

You are my favourite song to hear,
Removing all doubt, removing all fear,
Holding you close, holding you near,
You are my favourite song to hear.

You are my favourite sight to see,
Naked and beautiful, hair flowing free,
Holding you close, you touching me,
You are my favourite sight to see.

Stuart Stoter

EXPRESSIONS OF LOVE
(To Simon, my strength and stability, love always)

Belonging,
Everlasting.

Memories -
Yours and mine.

Valiantly, virtuously
Always aligned,
Lasting
Eternally.
Nurturing,
Tenderly,
In love -
Never
Ending.

Jacqueline Ann Johnston

I AM SORRY

I am sorry, I know you hate this word
Maybe more than you hate me
I am sorry, sorry for all the words I shed
I am sorry, sorry for all the pain I caused
I still remember every second I spent on you
The days you meant the world to me
The days I spent next to the phone
Days I forgot even those unending digits of pi
And the nights I spent dreaming of you
I stayed home waiting for your call
And you did call, every now and then
My every thought revolved around you
You never did anything on me
Despite all I did on you
You'll never be mine
But you'll always be there, deep inside
My love for you is like pi
Infinite, irrational and very important.

Hai Iam Shanu

TINDERSTICKS

Sometimes we touch in the deepest place:
It is not that blue and red make purple,
But that colour, freed of itself,
Can merge with the light.

Dee Rimbaud

THE DANGERS OF VERSE
(Dedicated to Joseph Stuart Kruse)

I shan't again write thee as the angel of my heart,
For 'tis thy mortal blood that doth stir all reason:
And poets know the fate of boasted words in art,
As conscious thoughts obscure in poems' treason:
Gospels of beauteous truth in verse are blistered,
For fear of such burial in my praise I dwell:
That in coffins of translation thy worth immured,
If in rich inflation I of thy exquisite lustre tell;
But, to simply read my thoughts in whispers,
To myself sweetly ensnared in memory's breath:
Life shall take in my mind's womb, messengers
Of profits full of envy for true immortal death.

In my verse's bloated greed, thy radiance dies,
Find thy glory here instead, behind my shaded eyes.

Shermin Izadpanah

COMPOSITION OF ROMANCE

Begin a new chapter with freedom of mind,
Do not rewrite, but write on a clean white leaf,
A lily-white page with the feelings you speak.
It is not easy for one whom is so closed and unread,
The challenge of life, living as one never has before,
But now realising the dream for which you have slept.

Sing with the words you so tenderly scribe in ink,
Let an angel take hold of the chords within your heart,
And make the music fly like doves with love in their eyes.
For it is only this music from the words that you write,
The melody of romance for which a story comes alight,
Paints a picture of lovers with one another . . . for life.

H Walsh

THE RAVAGES OF TIME

Memories lost between floorboards;
Placed safely in drawers;
Mislaid by time

Faces saved in shoe boxes
Forgotten names
Mislaid by time

Blank postcards banded together
Never sent from places abroad
Souvenirs of many travels
Journeys on life's winding road

Letters browning at the edges
Words of love in poetic lines
Secrets stored forever
To be mislaid through time.

Jessie Bruce

LOVE LOST

(Dedicated to Gene Kontos)

His kiss has a fire
His voice kills my ire
His touch has a passion
His hug has compassion
His arms hold me tight
His eyes give me sight
His heart gives me haven
His hair dark, like a raven
His love shines so bright
But he's not with me tonight.

Catherine Knapp

TO LOVE

Arrows, hearts, bluebirds and roses,
A kiss of the hand,
A kiss of the cheek,
Eyes meeting,
Hearts a fluttering.
Then a walk in the park with the sweet smell of spring.
A courting this shall be.

Then falling in love with a smile and a kiss,
A proposal, a ring, a celebration,
For summer a wedding there will be.

Flowing veils of white, petals and roses so red,
Bluebirds sing in trees of blossom so pink.
Hearts have been stung with passion and love.

Jenny Johnson

WITHOUT YOU

Your dreams burn hotter than the roaring sun
Your smile beams, soaring to the stars
In the brokenness of life
In the tears of goodbye
Gently the kisses you gave
Tender your touch did stay
At times I could not breathe
In your eyes my soul dreamed
If I was lost and in trouble
Your love embalmed me like a bubble
Softly floating, lifting high
Bursting in your arms, I cried

Al-Antony Moody

ICARUS WINGS
(For Vicky, my babe)

On the wings of Icarus
I fly.

I am risen up
by your touch
and your lingering taste
and your breath

I soar in your eyes
and swoop in your hair
I dive at your absence
and plummet at your despair

then I glide

as you smile

and on Icarus wings
I fly.

Shaun Allan

LOVE IS

L oving you is easy to do
O nly you know how deep and true
V ery special you are to me
E very day together we will be.

I t's there with me all the time
S pecial feelings, this love of mine.

Gill D'Arcy

WHAT WORDS CANNOT SAY

Roses are red
And violets are blue
This verse goes around and around
That is true

But with a woman as beautiful
As the one I now see
How can I put into words
What you mean now for me?

How can words so express
The passion I feel?
How can words so describe
The heartache you did heal.

But now I feel pain
For my heart it now shakes
I fear if I get closer
From this dream, I'll awake.

Words cannot tell
What I have to say
So I will just say,
'I love you.'

Happy Valentine's Day.

Philip Trivett

FIRST LOVE

He never knew how I felt
He who made my heart melt
A smile, the twinkle of an eye
I'd blush as he walked by
I dreamed of the day
When he would say
'I feel the same way too'

My love had the intensity of pain
I knew I'd never love again
Patiently I waited
Fingers crossed, breath baited
But the hand of fate
Left it too late
We moved on to other lives

The years passed and yet
I will never forget
I see him in town
Smile, speak, look down
In case he should see
The truth in me
Of how he broke my heart

Louise Wheeler

FOR SHIRLEY (MY DARLING WIFE)

A spider spins its silken thread
To make a place to rest its head.
A flower, reaching for the sun
Its petals wide, its life begun.
A bird that flies across the sky.
A child that asks the question why.
A tree, a field, a land of green
These are wonders I have seen.

But the most wondrous sight of all
Is not the bird, or tree so tall.
It's not the flowers that bloom so bright
Nor a child, or web so light.
None of these things that I describe
Can match my feelings deep inside.
Though I were blind I would still see
You love is all the life in me.

Martin Staton

PLEASE BE MY VALENTINE

The love I've always had for you,
is buried deep inside,
life has dealt us many blows,
from which I run and hide,
my anger comes when I am scared,
like the Devil in disguise,
if you are sure you just want me,
please be my valentine.

Audrey Lee

TO ROSIE

Oh, wild, wild Rosie, we've had no time,
To lie beneath the summer sycamore and lime,
But briefly walk down country lanes
And shelter from the autumn rain.

So little time to sing and laugh,
Along the leaf-strewn forest path,
And gaze upon the misty hills,
Where seasons mix and colours fail.

We've had so little time to dance and kiss,
A rush of words, a brief caress,
But share the sparkling city night
And sunset leaves ablaze with golden light.

John Feakins

COGNITION

You moved towards me
As I to you
And in that moment
Was recognition
We smiled at one another
In the communion
Of silent understanding
Our thoughts embraced.
In a lightning flash
Of burning bliss
Love had taken us in his fire.
And so I came enchanted
And tuned my heart to yours
In the fulfilment of
Mind and flesh
And the joy that is part of it.

Idris Woodfield

DESPERATE FOR LOVE!

She had beauty, she had charm
She had elegance, she had grace
She oozed confidence, looking calm
A permanent smile etched on her face.

She stood still in the store, looking around
Her rich red lips caught my eye
The girl of my dreams I'd finally found
Perhaps she could see I was very shy.

Her perfume had reached my senses
I was totally overcome, by the scent
She had managed to penetrate, my defences
I wanted to pay her a kind, compliment.

Her jewellery sparkled, like the sun
Her eyes, were as blue as the sky
She needed someone, to show her, some fun
And I was desperate, to be that guy.

Other chaps were giving, her a glance
You have to admit, they had great taste
One guy, was so nervous, drinking wine, from France
But it was his time, he was going to waste.

Her hair seemed to be, a silken thread
If I didn't move soon, someone else might
Don't be rude, course I didn't aim, to get her into bed
Well, maybe, but perhaps on another night.

I thought about the pictures, or even a meal
An evening spent, in the local wine bar
A night at the disco, didn't make much appeal
Or a trip to a beauty spot, in my sports car.

When I asked her, I had a red face, noticed people looking on
                                                    with a grin
I rushed out of the store in great disgrace, I'd chatted up a mannequin!

B W Ballard

MY GRANDMOTHER'S WEDDING RING

(My valentine for my wife Valerie)

I am sitting on my veranda, looking over my vast property
Thinking back to the time and the ways things used to be
To the time I thought I had found true love in the past
It was to be my one and only love, to forever last
I told her I had no money, and I worked hard for my pay
Working noon to midnight, twelve hours every day
Told her I could not give her, fancy clothes or anything
Only my love forever, and my grandmother's wedding ring
She had another suitor, he was old and fat and owned a lot
He was married, but he could give her what I could not
Telling her he would put her, in a fully furnished fancy flat
She said that she loved me but, after all, that was that
I remember her beauty, a great figure with all her charms
Then I found her one day, in that other man's arms
Packing my bags, as she tried to bar my way
I said that I would remember her, until my dying day
A few years later I met a girl and right away I could see
That she was different, she wanted naught but me
I took her hand and we left, to go far away over the sea
Before we left I said, that I owned just one single thing
But she could have, my grandmother's wedding ring
Now twenty-two years later, she sits by my side
I ask if she has been happy, since she became my bride
She looks at me and our sons, nineteen and twenty-one
Smiling she says, 'Look at them, remember all we have done.'
I ask if she wants new clothes, diamond rings or anything
She smiles and says, 'Only your grandmother's wedding ring.'

F K McGarry

MY SWEETHEART

Stars glittering in the sky
As slowly the time goes by
The moon is moving slowly
And the landscape is so lovely

The warmth of your hands around me
Makes your love simply surround me
Whispering sweet nothings in your ears
I can do for years and years

You swing your hair sideways
Matching your eyes rolling sideways
A body language so romantic
Making me feel so frantic

You twist your body as if to music
Believe me it is so classic
You laugh so gingerly
While I hold you tenderly

Our passionate kiss is such bliss
The opportunity I dare not miss
I look into your eyes so bright
Through the flickering candlelight

With red roses on the table
It is like a fable
The diamond ring I have in my hand
With bended knees I leave in your hand

I shall hold your hand and look into your face
As we talk about our happy days
Soon church bells will be ringing
And a large choir singing.

Albert Moses

CALIFORNIAN BABE ON MY MIND

Golden-haired babe
With LA smile
Brown-eyed angel
Shimmering in the Californian sun
Sexy legs and ruby-red lips
You left me breathless
Addicted to your love

In the Mojave desert
We sealed our vows
Kissed and snuggled
The whole night through
Hand in hand
Heart to heart
We savoured the taste
Of midnight love

Pacific blue
Warm waters divine
Blended our hearts
As we tasted sweet wine
Hispanic welcome
Te amor my bride

Frisco sounds
Clasp in your hair
We dined on Mexican
Castanets filled the air
Promises fulfilled
Designed for two
Californian babe
I love you true

Peter Paton

MY DECEPTION

Is he worth it?
What is his crime?
I could think of many deeds
If my heart only had the time
Yet I have time
To mumble and howl like a child
See reminders of you in everything
Letting it unnerve me for an eternal while
That little leap you feel
In your gut
Lost inside
Seeping through your veins
As old and tired as a century
I find myself anxiously waiting for something
These visions bring you back
I come alight again
This fuelled flame
They give me peace
Make me whole
Ever so briefly
A turn of the head
And it's gone again

Bryony Freeman

MY VALENTINE

The fourteenth of February, Valentine's Day,
This date for me was supreme,
But on quite a different theme,
It was my late wife's birthday,
Which therefore did hold sway,
Celebrated together for fifty years,
Not designed to bring forth tears;
Memories might do that now,
If allowed, but for the vow
To respect that date each year,
Though she's no longer there to share.

A life of love, with results,
Three children, and no insults,
They in turn did add to the scene,
Seven grandchildren in-between,
Six boys and a girl,
With them love does unfurl
And spread to embroil
So many more who toil,
For without it, life would be sad,
At least for this one grandad.

George Beckford

To My One, True Valentine . . .

We've now known each other for a very long time,
And each time we've met's been completely sublime;
From that very first time, all nervous and jumpy
To the sublimest of moments of divine rumpy-pumpy!
Days of reflection, nights of pure bliss -
With exquisite lovemaking which starts with a kiss;
I love being near you, to feel you so close -
To nestle against you, your face, cheek and nose;
To slowly undress you, reveal your soft skin,
To respond to your invite, and ease myself in.
To feel you surround me, so warm and inviting,
Making love with you, darling is very exciting.
You arouse me with love, and with smile and with touch,
When we're locked in embrace then I love you so much:
But I'll love you for always - till the end of all time;

For you are my true love - my dear valentine!

Anon

The Long Night Of Parting

It's morning at last
Ruffling through the dark
Midnight fears that fester in the mind.
The cold sweat and tears
Of love gone to waste
Lie dry on the pillow.
The goodbyes have been said
And delirium is now
A thing of the past.
The mind awakes.
It's morning again
And the long night of parting is over.

S Sreedharan

THE VOW

It was supreme, a perfect dream,
As I recall it now.
That lovely day, that special way,
We made our solemn vow.

You had my heart right from the start,
All those years ago.
It was so dear, it was so clear,
We loved each other so.

I promised you that I'd be true
And only death would sever.
Yet though I'm left alone, bereft,
My love goes on forever.

My heart is cold with none to hold
As I held you before.
Each night I miss your tender kiss
And love you even more.

Frank Jensen

OUTDOORS' VALENTINE

Flowers of frost on the windowpane
Puss willows dusted with rime
A robin flitting across a barrel's rim
Icicles fringed across the winter's barn
Silver clouds soft as the down
A hush as the evening descends
Beauty as nature only knows how

Carole A Cleverdon

A VALENTINE FOR A GENTLEMAN

Our gentleman's girl must be a beauty,
Not just any female cutie!
Our gentleman friend is not a very patient waiter,
So she must be special, for him to date her.
Golden hair down to her shoulder,
Or cut very short, appearing bolder,
Complexion just like cream and peaches,
Almost out of human reaches.
Her figure made to give no quarter,
Enough to fetch young ducks off water.
We certainly have no wish to alarm her,
But where do we find this female charmer?
Where is this modern 'Helen of Troy'
Who would make our gentleman friend a very happy boy?

G E Haycock

WHEN I AM WITH YOU

The darkness of the world
Disappears into nothingness
When I am with you.

The doldrums of life
Sail out to sea
Then disappear into
Its endless waves
When I am with you.

And my heart moves
Like a Beethoven sonata
Gracefully . . . softly
When I am with you.

Elizabeth C Millar

I Love You

Hold me and don't let me go
Let me feel your touch throughout my soul
Your gentle lips upon my face
Your warm body holds me close
The touch of your hands make me shiver inside
I close my eyes and feel so alive
As I look deep into your eyes like blue oceans
That I would cross to know you're on the other side
I sink deeper into your touch
Your gentle words lift me up to dance on the clouds above
So high, I feel, so in love once again
Just thinking of you, it drives me insane
I love you deeply, I love you so much
I love you forever and you're all that I want.

Tracey Bailey

Be My Valentine . . .

I tried to tell you 'I love you'
I tried to show it in every way
But you never got the message
So I hope you do this Valentine's Day

Do you remember what I told you?
Do you remember what I said?
I whispered it in your ear
Please tell me you didn't forget

I want you to be all mine
I want you to love me too
So please be my valentine
Because I am in love with you

Sonila Reka

DANDELIONS ON TOM'S CYBER GRAVE

It was supposed to be a comedy/drama
not this wretched tragedy
no one goes on at 25
not one with such talent
fluffy hair/chubby cheeks and adorable, wide blue eyes
we never even talked
just sneaked a glance
but I had hope
we were going to be
like Kenneth Branagh and Emma Thompson
maybe not as rich
and we certainly wouldn't have gotten divorced
fate laid other plans
now you're with Mark Frankel
talking of real acting and vampire princes
while I cry till my eyes itch
thinking how your favourite Tony Hancock got it right
Sundays will always be
rainy, uninteresting and endless

Nikky Ingram

UNTITLED

Memories on this special day
of love that has just passed
the feeling of your tender touch
the light reflecting on your champagne glass

Remembering the first time
i knew you were the one
butterfly nerves in my stomach
and 'us' had only just begun

So many wonderful moments
all equal to the rest
each thought just makes me glow inside
but which one is the best?

Let's celebrate our life my love
another precious day is here
how wonderful you are to me
happy Valentine's my dear . . . cheers!

Genevieve Anais

TRUE LOVE

There is a person special to me,
My heart goes to him for the world to see,
He makes my heart skip a beat,
Even more when we finally did meet.

I know deep down I love him so much,
His heart in my hands I want to clutch,
I never want to ever let go,
I love him even more so.

So baby I am talking to you,
Please don't let me feel blue,
I love you deep from in my heart,
Forever, together and never part.

So will you love me like I love you?
Thinking of me in all you do,
I know where my heart is going,
Out to you I am now showing.

My hand's in yours as we walk around,
Holding on tight to the love I've found,
As two hearts gel from two to one,
Our love together finally cut on stone.

Kerry Snow

YOU

I think of you,
during the early morning stumbles.
I think of you,
with that first glorious mug of coffee . . .
While involved in road-raged rush hour,
I am thinking of you . . .

I think of you,
during the earning hours.
I think of you,
amidst the customer bustle . . .
I think of you,
while conquering the lunch hour hustle.
While I swallow a cold cup of tea,
I am thinking of you.

I think of you,
during the wind-down to the weekend.
I think of you,
with the taste of red wine on my tongue . . .
When your hand slips into mine . . .
When your voice whispers, 'I love you . . .'
Even then, I'm thinking of you . . .

Samantha Braum

SAFEST HEARTS

You know who you are,
Your beauty so pure,
Your lips untainted,
The sweetest lure,
The softest skin,
And eyes so clear,
You're in my heart,
Forever you're here,
The kindest tongue,
The purest voice,
The safest arms,
Forever my choice,
I just want you to know,
I'll forever be true,
Always together,
Because Scott, I love you,
And after the dark night,
Comes the lightest day,
And I know you'll still be here,
Tomorrow and today.

Gemma Mackay

LOVE'S DAY

How soon the rosy dawn of desire's spring morn,
Succumbs to the blistering intensity of passion's long summer day.
Until the lengthening shadows of love's autumnal eve,
Describe eternal patterns in the gloom of melancholic night.

Damian Allen

LAWRENCE

I love you not
Just on this day
But every minute
In every way.

Before I sleep
And when I wake
All of the day
My thoughts you take.

You light my life
And make me whole
You have my heart
My very soul.

So on this day
My valentine
Forever yours
As you are mine.

Suzanne Thorne

TO MY VALENTINE

O sweet my lady whom I only love
When may I walk with you in the grove,
Loving you much and so much?

When will you walk with me in the grove,
Your hand in mine like a treasured trove,
Loving you truly and, softly to prove,
Kissing you much and so much?

When will you walk with me in the grove
Loving me much and so much?

Godfrey Ackers

WHAT IS LOVE?
(For Paula, my wife, my strength, my everything)

Love is a smile
That can melt the heart
It is happy and bright
An important part

Love is a touch
When a word won't do
It's that tender caress
When your world seems through

Love is a whisper
That floats on the air
No need to announce
You know that it's there

Love is a trust
For two to share
It's an understanding
That you'll always be there

Love is a child
That came from the heart
And moved me to tears
At a brand new start

Love is so real
With you at my side
You bring me reason
And a warmth inside

Love knows no limit
To a heart so true
Love is forever
For love is you

Tony Hucks

THE EYES OF MY VALENTINE...

I will look within your eyes
And behold the heart beating within;
In that essence is truth revealed.
The condition of your humanity
As upon a stage displayed;
In closest intimacy will I know you.

Each day I look for the sun
Burning with fierce determination
In eyes that reflect
Your joy, your happiness.
On those days of bleak despair
No ray escapes your core
The fears of past, present
No future in your darkened sadness.

Each day I look for the sun
To bask in the love displayed
Feeling the radiant energies of life well lived
Eyes that sparkle in a humour and with lust.
When thick, black clouds hide your heart
The pain is etched on eyes without lustre
Glittering only from the tear of anguish
The crushing pressure of hopelessness.

I will look within your eyes and read your story there
All victory and defeat; a clear imprint in the language of all worlds.
And behold the heart beating within; in that essence is truth revealed.

Robin Colville

THE INSPIRATION

(Dedicated to Teddy Bear)

Kiss me now, and bring me round
Touch my lips, don't make a sound
Reawaken the inspiration
Don't let me go to ground

Lift me up, and set me free
Hold me there, and let me be
Make it good, like good friends should
In the silent eternity

No need to speak, just be here
You and me, have no fear
You're my light, you're out of sight
The inspiration, dear.

Melinda Penman

HEART TO HEART

Heart upon heart
I give you my love

Holy upon holy
I give you my love

Stars and rainbows
Blessings of song

Divine to divine
I give you my love

Soul to soul
I give you my love

Man and woman
Blessings of one

Amelia Amy Peterson

UNTITLED

These warm feelings inside my heart,
Grow stronger each day,
You helped me through the tough times,
You've been there for me through the good times,
There is no one else I want to be with,
There is no one else who I love more,
I want to marry you baby,
So what do you say?
I know we're young but so in love,
On Valentine's Day,
I will treat you like a king,
I will be your willing slave,
As long as you're beside me,
I will be whatever you want me to be,
So do me the honour of becoming my husband.

Lucy Rushen (17)

WISHFUL THINKING?

I see your face where'er I look,
my heart reads like an open book,
a story of love, forever true,
a tale of feelings just for you,
this love I feel will last forever,
away, long past the twelfth of never,
I pray your heart can sing in tune
bringing us together, very soon,
then we could become lovers in life,
and finally, a man and his wife.

D T Pendit

DREAM

Let it be the snow
floating down
on the grey concrete floor outside,
melting as it hits each paving block,
parachute landing as it gently separates to water slush.
Let it be the sound of pitter-pat hailstones,
bouncing to and fro,
across the cold, hard land.
Let it be my hand as it reaches out
to touch the white, soft flakes,
wilting in my palm,
trickling down my arm.
Let it be your smile
blazing through the winter sky,
framed in the memory of swaying sound.
Let it be your heart
that beats closer
and warmer
as the snow falls outside.
Let it be your hand
holding mine,
not letting go,
completing my dream.

Marina Trowell

AN UPCOMING VALENTINE'S DAY

In less than a month's time
It'll be the day that lovers claim for themselves
Cupids with arrows
All the romantic crap

Many look forward to it in hope
Some act like it's another day
Others plan months in advance
I, however, am saddened by this prospect

This upcoming Valentine's Day
For me, symbolises loss
The last I'll spend with someone I love
The last I'll be anywhere near him

The loss, I guess, would sadden me less
If we could only speak
Even for a minute, maybe two
This, however, is too much to ask

Valentine's Day, a day for lovers?
I'd argue it was a day for loneliness.

Saara Mahomed

ON THE RED LIGHT

The consummate professional:
Chatting, to put me at my ease.
Gently he helps me to prepare:
Attentive - then deftly prompting,
Questioning - polishing my speech.

And I feel fine: with thoughts marshalled,
My favourite phrases practised, checked,
I'm eloquent and in control.

'I think we're ready now,' he says,
'We're rolling when the red light shows.'

And on the red light thoughts escape,
Eloquence evaporates as
I become a stuttering wreck -
Tongue almost tied . . .

                    Always on the
Red light it's the same: confidence
Withers, lines are fluffed, the simplest
Truth stays lodged in my dry throat.
Always at these times I need my best -
Instead, thick-tongued, I croak, whisper
All of life's most important lines
Like . . . 'I love you, love you, love you'.

Patrick B Osada

LINES ON MY CAT HARRY (A FELINE VALENTINE)

She is a line of black and liquid light
Which slides in at the window past the moon,
Then purrs the blues to me throughout the night.

I may awake to sounds of lust or fight:
Catcophony that some might call a tune.
She is a line of black and liquid light

Whose presence blends the senses - touch and sight
With hearing. When I stroke her, very soon
She purrs the blues to me throughout the night.

This warm, melodic nearness seems so right
But then she's gone - a ghost in moon and gloom.
She is a line of black and liquid light

And answers not to human love or might,
Yet her dismissive, independent mood
Still purrs the blues to me through day and night.

My life, just like my linen, was once white
But now her paws print both with careless runes
To tell me she's a line of liquid light.
My black cat purrs the blues throughout the night.

Vance Roberts

MY FIRST LOVE - FOR STEVIE

I've been in love that's unrequited, and it's highly overrated
I've loved not wisely but too well and that's simply living hell
I've been mistress to a toad and once is too often down that road
Old man's darling and young man's mother, really it's not
worth the bother
French man, German, Irish, Brit - think they're different? Not a bit.

Until at last, who'd have guessed? I found a love that's truly blessed
And if you think that you can keep it, I'll let you in upon our secret
He pursued and I resisted, unrelenting he persisted
I thought I'd had enough of lovers, that he'd be like all the others
Offered friendship, called his bluff, but he's made of sterner stuff

Thought he saw a sparkle in me, took his chance to woo and win me,
Slowly, slowly catchee monkey - till I craved him like a junkie
Till I learned the truth about him, till I could not live without him
Till unable to disprove him, I admitted that I love him
So what truth did I discover from this gentle king of lovers?

East needs west and sour needs sweet, otherwise they're incomplete
Unbalanced love cannot be true, for love's not love that's all askew,
He's the thought that now completes me, I go halfway,
he's there to meet me
I share his joys, he lifts my sorrows, we share all our unborn tomorrows
All this I have learned and more - I learned I've never loved before

Chris Johnston

A Cynical Look At February 14th!

We owe a lot to Valentine
We have to write a loving rhyme
And read a lot of silly verse
I'm not quite sure which bit is worse!

And give your love a single rose
On one knee perhaps propose
And hope that blushing flower so red
Will entice your love straight into bed!

Let's not forget the satin heart
Declaring, 'We shall never part'
Until at least the following day
When someone better comes to play!

Corks are popping, champagne bubbles
The world retreats, forget your troubles
Candles cast a tender light
You dance and sing till late at night

But in the sober light of day
Your senses return to you and say
That vision for whom you'd cross the road
Has turned into an ugly toad!

Celia Jackson

VALENTINE LOVE

Valentine's Day will soon be here
The day lovers wait for all the year
When a special card is sent to the one you love
Love is God's special gift sent from above.

It's a time to give flowers or maybe chocolates too
To show your love to that 'special one' - so easy to do
Perhaps an unexpected outing will be your surprise
Whatever it is - it will open your eyes.

In days gone by, a valentine card was not signed
Just the words 'from an admirer' sent with you in mind
But the best part of all was finding out *who*
This was much more exciting and easy to do.

Marjorie Ridley

THIS IS LOVE

At twenty I thought I was in love
That didn't last long, my love was abused
I suffered a massive broken heart
Which took years to mend
Until I found you, friends we became
It didn't take long for Cupid to hit me
With his arrow of love
A love that is passionate, tender, caring
Sharing and understanding
One where we say sorry if we've been hurt
One where we laugh and have fun
Tender moments when I know you are the one
Love is so many things
I've sampled them all in you
Andrew, my valentine

T R Chester

SLUSHY, GUSHY, LOVESICK PUPPY

I lost my love at sweet sixteen but now he has been found
For eighteen years have passed us by, I sense that we were bound,
The fires were still burning as he looked me in the eye,
My legs still weak and wobbly, my bits, well, me oh my,
He, he, haa, haa, what a lucky girl am I!

I think he'll have the best for me and me the best of him
For we've grown in wisdom and knowledge,
Had fun and learned from our mistakes,
Them eighteen years a learning curve on how to get it
Right.

I'm sure we'll have some fights but the making up will sure be fun,
He makes my body feel alive, so now the job's been done,
I've been bitten by the love bug, wrapped up in that gushy stuff.
Least now after eighteen years of existing I can do some living,
For I am now officially
A slushy, lovesick puppy.

Maxine Coughlan

VALENTINE'S DAY

Valentine's is the perfect day,
To declare your love in a special way,
To show you care and get the chance,
To indulge yourself in love and romance.
Flowers, chocolates and teddies galore,
But Valentine's means so much more,
It's the day when lovers shouldn't be apart,
It gives them the chance to speak from their heart,
To give their sweethearts a wonderful feeling,
And shower them with kisses that leave them reeling,
It lets them declare to their valentine,
I love you forever, please be mine.

Natalie Westerman

MY SEPTEMBER STAR
(For Steve Owen, 25/1/05, St Dwynwen's Day (Welsh Valentine's Day!))

A party girl cut a swathe through town,
and each weekend she let her hair down.
Kissing the boys, never to stay,
leaving false phone numbers, then running away.
Swinging her long hair, putting on the style,
fooling most of the people, most of the while.
Till one rogue Saturday when out of the blue,
across a table, she saw and studied you.
An unplanned night, an astonishing sight,
the timing all wrong, the timing all right.
A first date, which completely blew her mind.
A kind, gentle person she never expected to find.
Imperfect like her, lost in their way,
unsure of what to do and to say.
Beset by insecurities, struggling to cope,
feeling a renewed sense of possibility and hope.
You were a mirror, in which she saw herself clearly,
she recognised your pain, and adored you so dearly.
As they embraced on a sofa, her heart went boom.
How did it get to be this wonderful this soon?
Difficulties arose, though the chemistry was strong,
but sadly you couldn't stay for very long.

You fill my thoughts and fill my dreams,
a boy like you cannot comprehend what that means.
You are handsome, flawed, special and unique,
and when I think of you my knees go weak.
I have evaluated my world, which now seemed so narrow,
till Cupid aimed straight at my heart with a bow and arrow.
You mean the world to me, my valentine, and my love flows deep,
let me kiss you again until you fall asleep.

Mary Carroll

FEELINGS

I missed you again, like two people on
Parallel sides of a mirror.
If I only knew what feelings you reflected
Mine are so clear, my transparent heart
Waiting for you.

Alas I know the rules; only looks,
They say so much our looks, yet that is all
It will ever be.

What crime shall be next?
Not even to chance you and I,
The unknown is a scary place, but can we not venture
It together?

I wish our fear could propel us together
Yet stationary we stay for now
A moment's embrace is an eternity
To feel so much and to not give us a chance
Is the real fiend.

Though I go on an exaggeration of adoring
The moments we have.
A bomb to drop I hear you say,
But an explosion of truth my darling.

A new season, year and living
Will the new-found transience show us how good
It could be?
So put me out of my misery
With a simple 'I do'.

Daniel Skerritt

MY TRUE LOVE

You are my special someone
Who captured my heart
Who leaves me feeling lonely
When we're apart.
My love is so true
So pure in sight
My knight in shining armour
Riding through the night.
So far away
Yet so near in my soul,
Together forever
Time never taking its toll.
Your smile is a picture
Of joy in my head
Your beating heart
Of rose so red.
A dove you are
Sent from above
My life with you
Together with love.
To be in your arms
Is my true dream
I will love you forever
A continuous stream.
You are so special
I love you so
Our love will never fail
For friend or foe.

Belinda Lavin

DRIFTING

Gracefully as I lay down amongst
The cornflower meadow
My senses heightened by linnet song.

My arms prostrate beside me
One minute passes as I close my eyes, blue skies
As far as my mind can see.

My heart is lifted by memories gone before
True loves I have shared
With my spirit and soul.

No wrong was done or meant to those
I have left behind on my journey through life,
The smell of sweet grass.

I have asked nothing but to be loved
As I have loved.
Nothing given but myself, not to own.

To be blessed with this gift of heightened senses
To some may be a curse,
We must go forward.

It is not for us to choose our destiny
As the universe has already taken the path
For us to follow.

And though sincere there will be pain
To accompany our passions, our lives,
Our loves, our tears.

Nicky Anderson

WHAT IS LOVE? (TRULY, MADLY, DEEPLY)

How to begin to describe it?
This elusive butterfly called 'love',
It appears in all different disguises,
And surrounds us - below and above.

It's around us but completely invisible,
And without it we would not be here,
It's emotional yet also so physical,
And it conquers both hatred and fear.

It comes and goes as it sees fit,
And is deeply and madly addictive,
With its arrows it reaches its target,
Till we all become truly afflicted!

We all try to seek it externally,
It can cause us a great deal of pain,
But we need to search harder internally,
If true love we are hoping to gain.

Some have had it forever but don't know it,
And some have never known it at all,
Some have it but are unable to show it,
Some lose it when out of love they do fall.

Some steal it, some hide it, some share it,
Some hoard it and some give it back,
You can see it and feel it and touch it,
But to 'live' it involves quite a knack.

It's a spiritual channel of energy,
And we need to tap into its light,
It is *life* itself, given freely,
And without it, we'd give up the fight.

Philippa Howard

SEASONS
(For Liz)

I love you as the summer and the sun,
I love you as the hills, the open space,
I love you for your friendship and your fun,
I love you as the soft wind on my face;
I love you as the misty rain, the frost,
yes, love you as a field of driven snow,
still loving you through growing pains, the cost
of sudden storms that only lovers know;
I've loved you through the seasons and the years
(in love you offer me, so loving twice),
I'll love you through our laughter and our tears,
the salty with the sweet, the lovers' spice:
I'll love you, in God's love, while I have breath -
will *you* love *me* in life and after death?

Michael Brueck

CONSTANT
(To my still shy suitor JB, a little annual ceremony that means so *much)*

A blush upon his cheeks,
Looking up through his persistent fringe,
Squirming toes turning in his shoes.
Behind his back, a crackle -
Twisting fingers threatening damage
Until with a thrust and mutter
And embarrassed public kiss on cheek,
My valentine rose is held out.
And this one is really special,
As always,
For this is number forty-nine;
The first a crisp whisper
Lovingly preserved and pressed
Within my bedside Bible.

Di Bagshawe

THE WAY IT IS (PART 2)

You are black,
I am white,
I am your day,
You are my knight.

Time together
And conversation,
The source of all
My inspiration.

Giving me strength,
Always my rock.
My journey continues
But you're still my dock.

Tried to let go,
Can't break free,
Locked you in my heart,
Then lost the key.

Never a flicker,
Burning bright,
Forever dancing,
The moth round the light.

Gill Bestwick

MY LOVE

(Dedicated to my husband, Ronny - the love of my life)

Do you remember the day we wed
And all the vows that we said?
Do you remember the glorious sunshine
The day you said you would be mine?
Remember when the girls came along
They enhanced our love and made us strong
All the dogs and puppies too
We're slightly insane, me and you
Remember when times got tough
The sad, the bad and tragic stuff
They're all a part of me and you
We stuck together and we got through
25 years down the line
I'm still in love with that man of mine
Valentine's Day we celebrate now
Sometimes we may wonder how!
As years go by our shell may change
But inner feelings remain the same
I love you, you know I do
My life is pointless without you

Paula Burke

OUR LOVE

I lit a few red candles and sprayed perfume incense,
To sparkle our night of passion of romance.
Wearing my little black dress and wearing a thong,
Listening and dancing to our favourite love song.

We both sat down to a romantic meal,
Our love that we both show is for real.
We sit together by an open-logged fire,
Hoping to grow old together until we retire.

This is a poem I write and dedicate to you,
To appreciate the love, care and help that you do.
We've put away our emotional scars,
Placing your arms around me, we glance at the stars.

I wish I could collect for you the stars tonight,
The distant crystal moon shines a light
The moon represents the light of your soul
Feelings run wild of passion we can't control.

Your heart is the warmth of the golden sun,
You're my sacred and desired one.
I turn to lay my head upon your chest,
Spending time with you is cherished and my best.

You softly caress my long dark hair,
Treating me as an equal when sat in a wheelchair.
You present in your hand a beautiful red rose,
Then you drop on your knees to propose.

The answer is yes, you're constantly on my mind,
You're thoughtful, gentle and kind.
You're my only true valentine,
My heart filled with your love that always shines.

Lisa Madigan

A SWEETHEART

A face to win my heart is so hard to find
from myriads of faces that peeks
at the peak of needs or trough of times.
From the dark corner of my desire
a beacon of search shall rise to focus
upon my notion of quest for a sweetheart.

Could that unique gesture of hers be lost
in the mishmash of the web of wills?
And her enticing face just hidden
in the depths of my desire.
Where my heart sinks deep inside
in the pool of her platonic love.

At ease and peaceful I may look
but there is a storm of scarce faces inside.
This hunger, for one look of hers
one day will steal all my zeal of life.
So restless I am dying to seek
a lifelong hold of forsaken love.

Age of 'To you . . . from me' has gone past.
Time is now to say this once and for all
that she is the one I long to be with
and I will give up all I have and everyone.
So now is the time to come face to face
and be my valentine this year and forever.

Mojibur Rahman

THE JOURNEY
(To my husband)

The wheels shuttle loudly along the polished floors of the vacuum.
Voices echo near and far; voices of nurses, anaesthetist and
surgeons waiting,
For the endless trains carrying life's casualties,
On a journey through barren landscapes and desolate valleys.

I am just a statistic, someone's wife, mother and daughter.
I have consented to giving my body over to the voices.
With a glimmer of hope; that they might save me,
From the cruel savage beast of my generation.

My endless questions without answers have ceased,
And my tears are reflected; in the deep blue pools of your eyes.
My life and all which I hold dear, is set to be taken away.
Hold my hand tightly, till the fear subsides.

I sap your strength as I cling desperately to your hand,
And the train gathers speed and momentum.
We are sucked into the vortex of fear, pain and despair,
Heading towards its destination, the abyss.

Voices replace the darkness in my clouded eyes,
And glimpses of lucid reality rise to the surface;
I feel your presence; loyalty and love, as your hand envelops mine,
Warm and comforting, like a shawl on a cold day.

Life's experiences are not only etched in creases and lines
on my face,
They are carved across my heart; and the breast of my womanhood
has gone.
What you see is what I truly am now,
The vision you embraced, not shunned.

Our futures are uncertain but we are out of the vortex,
Living for the moment; life with all its uncertainties and frailties,
Will not blight our love which is certain and strong,
Thank you my darling for holding my hand and loving me.

Sharon Valentine

YOU'VE BROUGHT ME THIS FAR
(For Victor)

In my poetic mood tonight
I want to write and let you know
that I feel for you a joy
that no one else can give to me
a lovely feeling of peace
and relaxation flows
from your jolly ways
your interesting mind and your
masculine body of delight.
It is great to sit and talk
or lie beside your body
when I feel that emptiness
that life can give to me
but when I meet you
it disappears quickly
as your wit and joy help me
when all else has failed
and hopeless mornings
turn to moments of ecstasy
in my tiny room,
life is not so bad just now
stay beside me if you can.
I'll try to make
no demands on you
I cannot help it if I do,
it is the way I feel about you
so please understand
I am another human being
with a soul of love
crying out in my deepest needs
on this St Valentine's Day.

Mary Guckian

THE SOCK

I walk in the door at 5 o'clock,
Into the hall and pick up a sock,
Straight up the stairs, and make the bed,
Must hurry up, we need to be fed.

But! find on the floor,
More! screwed up clothes!
So, fold them and tidy,
This room I do loathe.

Collect the glasses,
And take down the mugs,
But! pass the bathroom
'Is that a new rug?'
No! it's a towel, wet on the floor!
And a pair of old boots behind the door!

So, try to carry all this down the stairs
Oh no! the hoover is still sitting there!
Walk into the living room
Where I find another top!
Oh no! not more clothes, I hope that's the lot.

But! I find old newspapers all over the floor,
Now into the kitchen where I find more -
Rubbish to clear and plates to scrape,
Unload the dishwasher! Dinner will be late!

Reload the dishwasher, then feed the cat,
Turn around and see *more* crumbs on the mat!
So, pick up the broom and sweep them up!
Then look in the freezer,
What can I muzzle up?

Defrost the curry I made the other night,
Stick on the rice, ready for tonight.
Now, dinner is on, I can sit down for a while,
But no! The cat screeches and lets out a cry!

She stands by the door, then wanders about,
Does she want to stay *in,* or want to *go out?*
It makes me envious, would I like to be a cat?
But a *husband's role* must beat that!

Although I shouldn't complain,
He does help me out,
But! only after I nag and shout!
When he helps out he really does try,
In fact, he does a better job than I.

But that's not what I want, for me to be a pest.
I want *him* to do it, when he *knows* I need a rest!

To open that door at 5 o'clock!
To see *him* picking up that old sock!

Telling me to sit down and making me a drink,
Then go into the kitchen and feed Dinks (the cat)
Putting on the dinner, then serving it up on a plate!
Would be great!
Then running me a bath, so *I can unwind,*
Whilst he clears the plates and go gets the wine.

Forget! The diamond necklace!
Forget! The expensive clothes!
For the best present you can give me,
Is a night that I have shown . . .

Karen Ferrari

CELESTIAL BODIES

And so it passes
like a shooting star;
a comet flashing
in the blackness
between the stars.

But then the moon
begins to rise.
Tonight it is full
and it fills the sky
with its light.

No marks are seen
on its façade;
it shines that brightly.
But they are there,
they cover its surface
on some nights.

And at other times
it's obscured,
either by cloud or
the changes time brings.

And sometimes it is
covered in blackness,
but the same
bright moon
is always there
behind the dark.

And it will never die,
this feeling,
stronger than the first.

Ricky Mitchell

AN ODE TO VALENTINE'S DAY

We rush down the stairs,
The postman has gone,
We look on the mat,
Something is wrong.

Just bills and reminders,
And junkmail galore,
No teddies or chocolate,
Or cards on the floor.

Nobody loves me,
Nobody cares,
No one to hold,
And no love to share.

But sat on the sofa,
With hair in a mess,
With baggy pyjamas,
I couldn't care less.

No groaning or moaning,
Or, 'What time is tea?'
We can eat what we want,
Just doggy and me.

So if you feel lonely,
On Valentine's Day,
Just smile to yourself,
And be glad it's that way.

Samantha Walsh

VALENTINE'S WISH FOR SIS

This poem may not be
in the true sense of Valentine's Day.
Still it goes to wish you
the best in life all the way.
To a girl who is yet to fall in love,
some piece of advice I'd like to say,
about boys and their ways.
Quite a funny lot. Aren't they?

Don't judge a book by its cover,
or a man by his colour.
For, he might lack the four Ms -
muscle, money, mansion and a Mercedes,
but to open the doors of your heart,
he might just be having the keys.

Don't go for the guy who says,
he fell for your style.
Take the one who says, 'of all your curves,
he was taken by your smile'.

His looks might impress you,
and far away you might hear wedding bells chime.
But his deeds must impress your heart,
for that's what makes love last a lifetime.

He must be a person whom you look up to.
Doesn't mean he should be six feet tall.
And if he makes you look and feel small,
your heart you might have to recall.

Whatever he be, of caste and creed,
his duty is to help you in times of need.
He must make you feel happy and gay,
and keep your sorrows and troubles at bay.

He must be caring enough to wipe your tears,
and help you get rid of your fears.
Then life will be a pleasant journey,
and you won't have to switch gears.

Love has its fair share,
of many a problem and pleasure.
I pray, the latter predominates,
when you find your treasure.

And when you are smitten by Cupid's darts,
keep it to yourself, don't let it part.
The charm of love lies in secrecy,
since it is only between two hearts.

Let the sky be your limit.
Be a pair of birds.
Thoughts are cramming up,
but I'm lost for words.

This flower beside might wither away.
To worms this page might fall a prey.
These words you might forget in a day,
but the message these words convey,
in your heart should forever stay.

Prasad Rajendran

CUPID'S BOW

Cupid when you draw your bow
Keep it straight and don't let go
Until your aim is straight and true
Or you may make someone very blue.

When that arrow starts to fly
I don't want to hit him in the eye
So aim for his heart right from the start
With that clever little golden dart.

Please remember I want him to be smart
I don't want just anyone to have my heart
And I need someone to fire my brain
Not someone who will always complain.

He must be strong but gentle, trusting and true
With a sense of humour to make me laugh when I'm feeling blue
Great looks are not essential as manners maketh the man
Someone with sensitivity, self-love and self-worth.

But I'm not quite sure if you'll find him on this Earth
The man who treats me with respect and not neglect
Can win my heart with or without that Cupid's dart
So where are all these sensitive interesting men?

Do I have to make one up using my pen?
And if I do will you Cupid, draw back your bow?
Make him real and true, go on, because
I long to hear him say and mean, *I love you.*

Rita V Goodhart

DECISION

I have thought it all out
And I refuse to accept
That it is trite and silly
To gaze at the moon
Thinking of you,
Hoping you look at the moon
Thinking of me.

After all, her beauty
Is not diminished
By the thousands of eyes
Which have gazed
On her strange face
Over the years,
Or her mystery lessened
By the millions of words
Sung in her praise.

Springtime is no less sweet
Because we rejoice
Seeing her come
Every year without fail,
The birds' songs
No less heartrending
Because they are ever with us.

So - I shall continue
To gaze at the moon
And think of you,
Hoping you do the same,
Thinking of me.

Helen Laurance

PERCY FRENCH SMILED DOWN ON US

We stood on the beach, the wind blowing in from the Irish Sea,
Ripples on the shore reminded me of a scene in a Desert Rats film,
It was bitterly cold but then again it was the middle of February,
We had chosen Newcastle, Co Down for our Valentine's treat.

The artist and poet, Percy French, once painted that bandstand
over there,
We'd a picnic there earlier as we sheltered from the winter breeze,
Brass bands don't play anymore but one can still hear their sounds,
Fading out into a cold winter afternoon.

There was a lot of romance back in the mid-eighteenth century,
Although Mandy and myself have still a lot of love in our hearts,
The mountains of Mourne like thousands of giants engulfed us,
With their warmth and humanity as we stood on that windswept beach,
The mist shrouded that sleepy seaside town as if we were on
Table Mountain.

We know it's not exotic and can sometimes be a little bleak,
But we've warmth inside us to stretch those five continents,
We heard there are some fantastic shells on these golden shores,
Which Mandy had come to collect in her little Fisherman Friend tin,
She may even find something exotic washed in from the Indian Ocean.

We searched for hours and walked miles looking in the shingle,
Someone let their dog off its leash and it charged down the beach,
It kicked sand in my face like a Charles Atlas buffoon, circa 1950.

It grew even colder now and the lights from the amusement arcades,
Flickered and twinkled like stars in the northern hemisphere,
I removed my coat and draped it over Mandy's shoulders,
We left the beach with a tin full of the most unusual shells
we could find,
Not into the arcades with their 'Penny Falls' and 'Cake-Walk'
machines,
No, we made our way to our favourite pub, Quinn's, warm and toasty.

Mandy took a seat by the shrine to George Best who looked
down on her,
As Percy French had done earlier, as we gathered shells on that
windswept beach.

Ben E Corado

LOVE

Love is just like glass, a beautiful fragile thing,
Look after it and nurture it, it'll make your heart sing.
If the glass is broken by uncaring deeds,
The love will wither and to divorce this leads.

My love is my woman, I have loved her then and still,
When she kisses and loves me it gives me such a thrill.
My wife is now my family, her cares are all mine,
Together we'll plant seeds in life's garden for all time.

My woman became my lover, my lover became my wife,
Some aren't this lucky throughout their whole life.
My love she really knows me, understands my moods well,
What I need to be happy she can always tell.

My wife's a clever woman, her choice of me was poor,
She could do so much better if she walked out the door.
I'm so glad she didn't leave me when things they were bad,
Now things are better we laugh at how little we had.

So now I end this poem,
Written for my loving wife.
I love you dear and need you,
And will do my whole life.

Sean Sessions

TAKE MY HAND, MY LOVE

Ride with me to Lemuria,
to lands of poet's awe;
we can race tonight on a fiery mount
for the hinterland of dream.
Take my hand, my love
and we'll sit astride
the milk-white steed of my soul.

Fly with me to Aurora,
to stars of shimmering skies;
we can whirl tonight on solar wings
for sacred suns of fire.
Take my hand, my love
and I'll raise you high
on the sinew of my mind.

Sail with me to Sargasso,
on élan's swirling tide;
we can surge tonight on a silver ship
to shores of lover's song.
Take my hand, my love
and I'll keep you safe
in the chariot of my arms.

Lay with me in Shangri-La,
in vales of green and gold;
we can soar tonight on a fervent breeze
to heights of love unknown.
Take my hand, my love
and I'll hold you close
in the Galahad of my heart.

Michael James Treacy

GIVE AND TAKE

Give to evil, give to good
Give me you and know you should.

Hold my torture, hold my soul
Hold your breath and breathe the cold.

Cease your anger, cease your fear
Cease the tears that brought you here.

Seize the moment, seize my hand
Seize the right to understand.

Bear the knowledge, bear your skin
Bear the flame that burns within.

Share this touch, share this night
Share these wings as you take flight.

Spare my mind, spare the seed
Spare this doubt that you don't need.

Feel the heat, feel the nerve
Feel my fright and heed the verve.

Live to dream, live to see
Live for now and thrive off me.

Keep your smile, keep your lust
Keep this love that turned to trust.

Beat the demon, beat the greed
Beat that heart that longs to bleed.

Take the darkness, take the pain,
Take my life,
And live again.

Elizabeth Toop

THE POSITIVE ASPECT

Of what use, but
If a beautiful flower
Does not possess
The element of fragrance.

View a lofted lotus
How delightful,
Attractive it looks
Even in a filthy pond.

Observe a honeybee
Which only collects honey
Without causing damage
To the beautiful flowers.

Likewise, should mind
Delight like a lotus
Though surrounded
By insatiable thoughts.

Gathering love thoughts
Reflecting sweet views
The positive feelings
Hid in every heart
Beautiful and bountiful,
Should evolve out
To script a positive future
Full of love, love, love.

T Ashok Chakravarthy

FIRST LOVE

Do you remember first love
Being hit by Cupid's dart
When you hugged each other
And vowed you'd never part

That magical feeling
As if you walked on air
The sky above was always blue
No dark clouds anywhere

You were so content and happy
And life was full of fun
You couldn't understand
Why some faces looked so sad and glum

And then what happened, you grew up
Was it all a dream
That faded back into the past
As if it had never been?

But memories come flooding back
And then you pause awhile
Remembering far-off carefree days
And in your heart you smile

May Morrott

MY LOVER

(Dedicated to my husband, David)

Sleep with me my lover,
Until the end of the night.

Hold me my lover,
I'll love your fears aside.

Need me my lover,
For I am the substance of life.

Touch me my lover,
I am all you want to feel.

Walk with me my lover
I'll support you through.

Breathe with me my lover
For you're all that I will ever need.

KJ

NIGHT VISIONS

In the heat-throb of summer you'd come to me,
Drifting in on the fragrance of June and July.
Beneath the flower-wreathed window, in lunar lambency,

The warm sandalwood wind tonguing my sweat-slicked skin,
Passion's perfume seeped through pores,
Love's heavy scent dried on my thighs.

You vanished in autumn, a rasp of dry leaves.
Now you appear in a sliver of streetlight, muted in moonlight;
The sour yellow rind of a thin moon, gone bitter.

Charlotte Leather

DESTINED LOVERS

In your presence I am blissfully smitten,
By the insect of passion I have been bitten,
Various letters to you I send stating, 'I love thee'
Into the crowd I don't intend to blend, I state persistently,
I differ from the others; I am not a swine,
I want nought but to win the affection of thine.

On your body I shan't pounce; a fierce glutton,
Until on your blouse remains but one button,
I merely yearn to kiss your lips,
And be caressed by your fingertips,
Others must be free of the knowledge for what we desiderate,
To be alone together; by the hand of fate,
Your eyes dart to my being; for others your desire plays possum,
The beauteous bud of our love does blossom.

Jamie Hogue (13)

IF YOU WERE . . .

If you were a book I'd never stop reading,
If you were a cut I'd never stop bleeding.

If you were time I'd want to stand still,
If I became ill you'd be my pill.

If you were a pen I'd never stop writing,
If you were a war I'd never stop fighting.

If you were my voice I'd never stop talking,
If you were my legs I'd never stop walking.

If you were a seed you'd grow every day,
If you were God, to you I would pray.

I am yours and you are mine,
Together forever our love will shine.

Lynsay Bestwick

Lovers' Lock

Wow, here I go again . . .
A captured glance,
a murmured delight.
Mmmm, to pleasures had,
and those to follow.
Hold hands, break hearts
trip over the tongue, that
speaks the unspoken.
Lovers whisper, tears lie.
A truth is told but never
the whole story.
Shallow thoughts but
too good to lose, an
imagination raring to go!
Feelings lie dormant but
release will soon follow.

Karen Roberts

I See You

I hold you in my mind
But it is not the bulk of your body,
Nor the curve from ear lobe to shoulder,
Nor the power of your sex,
Although I yearn for these,
And for more than the sum of all these.

But in my mind I see you
Waiting for me,
And my heart lifts at your expectant face.

Tessa Paul

THIS LOVE . . .

Open is the heart that feels,
So brisk the pain it tortures all.
Embedded is the knife, it bleeds for tender fools.
When morning takes the breath of babes
Enwrapped in cherubs' sleep,
The very reason for this love . . .
When in the shadows creep.
Angels watch for moonlight fades,
As beauty does in time.
Then spirits dance like glistening light
. . . As bells of midnight chime.
I'll never sleep without this love,
Or breathe without you near,
For all the seasons worship us,
Together without fear.

Marianne Bullen

THE SUPERGLUE OF LOVE

We all need love to keep us sane.
It's the superglue
that keeps us from disconsolation.

Love is the answer to tears and sorrow.
The bruising of heartbreak
when we think of tomorrow.

Love is the balm that soothes our pain.
It's the superglue
that keeps us from disintegration.

Maureen Reynolds

To My Love

My life is but a rainbow,
You are my pot of gold,
The bright and vivid colours,
Are the children we hug and hold,
You are my brilliant sunshine,
You are my everlasting light,
You are my special soulmate,
Shining to help in dark nights,
You give me love and happiness,
You care for all you know,
You emit an aura of gentleness,
Your tenderness makes my heart glow,
You are the one I'll always love,
And eternally will you know.
Thank you for our precious children,
Who now have children of their own,
You've kept this family close and strong,
So we will never ever be alone,
You've given me all I ever wanted,
And everything I could ever need,
A love so deep and perfect,
Cynics find it hard to believe,
You make me want to sing and dance,
You fill my heart with awe,
You make my spirit soar with joy,
And I'll love you forever more.

Celia Auld

VALENTINE'S DAY

I sent my love a valentine
And begged and begged her to be mine.
I know I've left it a bit late in life
To settle down and find a wife
But they say that where there's life there's hope
And I'll try that Viagra if I really can't cope.

She likes Wordsworth and Shelley, so I tried really hard
To write something literary to put in her card.
'With lots and lots of love and loads of kisses.
Please will you marry me, and then we'll be Mr and Mrs.'
Back came her reply - oh, woe is me!
I don't think she liked my poetry.

'I really, really do not care
About your lack of teeth - or hair.
I don't mind your pacemaker and plastic knee
I don't even mind that you're 83.
But I could never marry a man
Who writes poetry that doesn't scan!'

Marion Scourfield

IF ONLY

If only I were as thou art -
as pure in soul, as kind of heart;
as light of step, as whole a part -
if only I were - as thou art.

If only I could somehow be
gorgeous and radiant as she;
free as the air yet deep as the sea -
if only I could - somehow be.

If only I saw as she sees
the waving hay, the bustling bees,
the soaring lark, the tall dark trees -
if only I saw as she sees.

If only we stood and only we saw
the sun set 'neath yonder shore -
with the sky lit up with a crimson hue;
and just hear her say 'I love you'.

Edward Fursdon

THE TOUCH OF LOVE

A blind man could see
The effect you have on me.
The way I tremble at your touch.
My quickened breath is much
Too fast. Can my heart stand
This passion? Such thrills are only for the young
Or so I understand.
Have I been wrong perhaps?
Could it be, at our age
We have found true love?
Will these feelings last
Or will they grow cold
As dawn creeps through the window?
Will you go and leave me old
Crying in my pillow
Or will we spend our lives
Or that which is left now
Together, not cold, but warm?

Jane Manning

LOVER OF THE LOVELESS

The cross - how cruel!
Your lifeless body was gently carried to the tomb.
White linen and spices enthroned your lacerations;

Carefully placed, sorrowfully measured.
The stone at the entrance rolled in place.
All was quiet within but teardrops without.

The night came on, the Sabbath day began.
The hearts of all were uneasy;
Had they slain the Lord of Glory?
Was He the one who should redeem Israel?

Resurrection - what a glorious event!
On the first day of the week!
Jesus stepped forth from the tomb,
Conqueror over death and sin
A lover for all who will!

Alice Blackburn

YOU ARE MY LOVE

You are my pal, my confidante, companion
You give me hope when all is in despair,
When in the valley, raise me high to mountaintop
And build me up when no one else would care.
When through life's journey, hand in hand we'll travel
I'll tell the world I'm yours and you are mine (our love's divine)
Together overcoming toils and trials
In harmony, two independent lives combine.
I dread the dawn, when I am left without you,
If you should go and I am all alone,
And so each day you'll be my boast, my one desire,
Throughout the world, my love for you is known.
You are my friend, I dare not live apart from you,
My joy, my hope, the one whom I adore (I love you more)
You are my love, I'll cherish you eternally
And so each day, my dear, on you, my love I'll pour.

Colin Ross

INFORMATION

We hope you have enjoyed reading this book - and that you will continue to enjoy it in the coming years.

If you like reading and writing poetry drop us a line, or give us a call, and we'll send you a free information pack.

Alternatively if you would like to order further copies of this book or any of our other titles, then please give us a call or log onto our website at www.forwardpress.co.uk

Anchor Books Information
Remus House
Coltsfoot Drive
Peterborough
PE2 9JX
(01733) 898102